Sandra Lee
semi-homemade

Weeknight Wonders

This book belongs to:

_____

Solution-based

Enterprise that

Motivates,

Inspires, and

Helps

Organize and

Manage time, while

Enriching

Modern life by

Adding

Dependable shortcuts

Every day.

Published by John Wiley & Sons, Inc., Hoboken, New Jersey, in partnership with SL Books.

Published simultaneously in Canada.

Cover photo by George Lange; selected author photos by Jill Lotenberg

For general information on our other products and services or for technical support, please contact our Customer Care Department within the United States at (800) 762-2974, outside the United States at (317) 572-3993 or fax (317) 572-4002.

Wiley also publishes its books in a variety of electronic formats. Some content that appears in print may not be available in electronic books. For more information about Wiley products, visit our web site at www.wiley.com.

Library of Congress Cataloging-in-Publication Data
Lee, Sandra, 1966-
  Sandra Lee semi-homemade weeknight wonders : 139 easy fast fix dishes.
    p. cm.
  Includes index.
  ISBN 978-0-470-54024-4
  1. Quick and easy cookery. 2. Cookery, American. 3. Brand name products. I. Title.
  TX833.5.L397 2009
  641.5'55--dc22
                                                2009029986

Printed in the United States of America.

10 9 8 7 6 5 4 3

SL BOOKS
sandralee.com

WILEY

John Wiley & Sons, Inc.

sem·i-home·made

adj. 1: a stress-free solution-based formula that provides savvy shortcuts and affordable, timesaving tips for overextended do-it-yourself homemakers **2:** a quick and easy equation wherein 70% ready-made convenience products are added to 30% fresh ingredients with creative personal style, allowing homemakers to take 100% of the credit for something that looks, feels, or tastes homemade **3:** a foolproof resource for having it all—and having the time to enjoy it **4:** a method created by Sandra Lee for home, garden, crafts, beauty, food, fashion, and entertaining wherein everything looks, tastes, and feels as if it was made from scratch.

Table of Contents

Chapter 1

Dinner Delights
16

Chapter 3

Coast to Coast
60

Chapter 2

Asian American
38

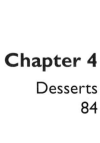

Chapter 4

Desserts
84

Dedication

To Mariah, Michaela, and Cara, my Semi-Homemade munchkins, for making every night an amazingly wonderful weeknight wonder full of adventures.

Letter from Sandra

My new book, *Semi-Homemade® Weeknight Wonders*, is a busy cook's best friend, offering a diversity of lightning-fast ways to whip up delicious dinners in less time than it takes to say, "Pizza, please." Packed with smart shortcuts and thoughtful advice, each chapter redefines home cooking, dishing up made-from-scratch taste with a fraction of the effort. You'll find months of money-saving meals, 139 fix-it-fast recipes for appetizers, entrées, sides, and desserts fashioned from ready-made, fresh, and frozen ingredients.

Every time I go to the grocery store or shoot one of my Food Network shows, I always search for fresh, doable everyday dinners that taste special, yet make the most of limited resources. When time and money are tight, the solution is my "Triple A Factor"—Accessible, Aspirational, and Affordable meals that anyone can make and everyone can enjoy. Each recipe starts with easy-to-find foods that make meal prep a breeze for even the busiest lifestyle. Meals are now budget-friendly, utilizing streamlined ingredients, in-season foods, and power-packed seasonings that deliver big flavor at a less-than-takeout cost.

For more money saving recipes, tips, and ideas, log onto www.semihomemade.com. Join my magazine family there too!

While we all welcome the weekend and the sense of leisure it brings, there's a whole week of days when leisure is elusive. We work long hours, then hurry home to get a hot, nutritious dinner on the table. Add shopping and cleanup to the to-do list and it's a wonder we have any time at all. *Weeknight Wonders* takes stress off the menu with simple, healthful recipes that require less time for cooking, so you have more time for sharing food and fun with family and friends.

Old favorites and new flavors come together in a melting pot of dinners that cater to every taste, from cozy American comfort foods to robust Italian, festive Mexican, and elegant Asian dishes that are an inventive fusion of classic and contemporary. Every chapter takes a culinary trip somewhere special, whether it's down South, through Cajun Country, across Middle America, or Coast to Coast, with regional specialties that make mealtime an adventure. Pair any entrée and side with a quick-fix dessert and you have a complete, well-balanced meal that pulls together with ease any night of the week.

Create wonderful home-cooked meals quickly and serve them with love, even on weeknights. It's more than doable—it's a luxury we can all savor and share.

Cheers to a happy, healthy home,

Sandra Lee

Simple Sides

Supereasy Serve-Alongs: Most of a busy cook's time and attention goes to the main course. Side dishes often get short shrift—and that's too bad because they truly do round out the meal. That's why I love the convenience of prepared dry rice and pasta sides. All you have to do is add water and a little butter or oil and cook on the stovetop or in the microwave. They come in a variety of flavor profiles to go with any main dish, whether it's American comfort food, or Italian, Asian, or Mexican. Frozen vegetable sides in flavorful sauces only have to take a quick spin in the microwave. Put either one in a pretty bowl and garnish with a little cheese or fresh herb, if you like, and you're good to go.

Really Quick Bread: A just-add-water corn bread mix lends itself to all kinds of experimentation. Make it plain—or flavor it with complementary stir-ins such as lemon zest and fresh blueberries, chopped kalamata olives and snipped oil-packed sun-dried tomatoes, or canned diced green chiles and grated sharp cheddar or Monterey Jack cheese.

Saucy Beans: Canned beans are low in fat and high in fiber and protein. If they come already seasoned, just heat and serve—or personalize them just a bit. Stir a chunky salsa—hot or mild, as you like it—into Southwestern-style beans. Or top creamy refried black beans with sour cream, cheese, and colorful red corn chips. Either one is delicious with grilled or broiled steak or chicken or quick tacos made with shredded slow-cooked pork shoulder.

Great Ingredients Your pantry includes cupboards, freezer, and refrigerator. Stock them well with fresh, high-quality ready-made, as well as dry ingredients, such as rice and sugar, and a delicious meal is always at hand.

Pantry Essentials Having fresh-from-the-oven baked goods any night of the week is really just a matter of having a pantry full of products such as convenient baking mixes, oils, and quality sugar that can make that possible.

Baking Basics: Quick Ideas

Beautiful Biscuits: A warm biscuit is welcome at almost any meal—but who has time to mix, roll, and cut the dough on a busy weeknight—not to mention the time to clean up the floury mess? Refrigerated biscuits make quick work of baking—and with no mess to boot.

Terrific Toppings: Your favorite casserole or hearty oven stew tastes even better crowned with a savory biscuit topping. Bisquick® baking mix makes it easy to try all kinds of fun flavor combinations. Consider stir-ins such as chopped fresh herbs, cracked black pepper and Parmesan cheese, or crisp-cooked bacon and shredded cheddar. Dollop one batch of biscuit dough on the hot casserole or stew the last 15 to 18 minutes or so of baking time or until the biscuits are golden brown.

Sweet Endings: Transform a sugar cookie mix into one of my favorite sweet treats—Sugar Sandies. When you mix the dough, stir in about $1/2$ cup finely chopped almonds or pecans, then generously sprinkle each cookie with granulated sugar (or roll balls of dough in sugar, if you prefer) before baking.

Sweet and Simple

Cool Ideas for Hot Cocoa: A simple cup of hot cocoa becomes dessert when it gets dressed up with a gorgeous dollop of whipped topping, a drizzle of chocolate syrup, and a sprinkling of chocolate chips, peanut butter chips, or milk chocolate toffee bits.

Sensational S'mores: You don't have to save s'mores for weekend cookouts—or for the school-age set. S'mores are so simple to make and the ingredients store in your pantry perfectly, so you can savor this sweet treat any day of the week and during any season. Try making them with dark chocolate bars rather than the usual milk chocolate. The rich, sophisticated flavor makes these childhood favorites special enough to follow any type of meal.

Kisses All Around: The combination of chocolate and peanut butter is irresistible. Classic Peanut Butter Blossom cookies are a cinch to make when you use a peanut butter cookie mix. Have your chocolate kisses unwrapped and ready so as soon as the cookies come out of the oven, you can press them into the center of the soft, warm cookies. Remove the cookies from the baking sheet to a wire rack to cool completely.

Chocolate Creations With just a few simple ingredients, you can feed your need for chocolate in a variety of forms: a frothy cup of cocoa, an ooey-gooey s'more, or a sweet PBB (that's Peanut Butter Blossom) cookie.

BEFORE

AFTER

Quick Nibbles and Sippers

Fashionable Food: Give a selection of savory Johnsonville® sausages a makeover into something fun to nibble with drinks. Try Italian Hot Links cooked, sliced, and speared on toothpicks with a hot pepper and Four-Cheese Italian Links with cubes of cheese. Cook and crumble Italian All-Natural Ground Sausage, then stuff into big fat beautiful mushrooms. Bake in a 425 degree F oven for about 10 minutes and serve. Make whimsical pigs-in-a-blanket with cooked bratwurst wrapped in crescent roll dough and baked until golden brown and crusty.

Merry Mocktails: For the drivers in the crowd—or for the guest who simply doesn't care to imbibe—these lovely sparkling drinks offer flair and festivity without alcohol. In a pretty flute glass, combine chilled sparkling white grape juice with chilled cranberry juice, lemonade, or orange juice—then garnish with fresh berries or a wedge or a twist of citrus.

Easy Entertaining Ready-to-pour cocktails that only require some ice, the perfect glass, and a few fresh and fanciful garnishes make weeknight gatherings simple and stress free. Friends will offer a toast to the savvy hostess.

Dinner Delights

As much as I have favorite dishes I've made many times, I delight in trying something new. Whether it's elegant Pomegranate-Glazed Duck or homey Gouda Mushroom Potatoes, there is something here to tempt you into the kitchen to try a new taste.

Tomato Garlic Short Ribs

Prep 10 minutes   **Cook** 3 hours   **Makes** 6 servings

4   pounds beef short ribs

        Salt and ground black pepper

2   tablespoons vegetable oil

2   large carrots, peeled and chopped

1   stalk celery, chopped

2   tablespoons chopped garlic,
        Gourmet Garden®

1   can (10.7-ounce) tomato purée,
        Hunt's®

¾   cup cognac or brandy

1   cup dry red wine

2   packets (1.25 ounces each)
        peppercorn gravy mix, *McCormick*®

3   cups lower-sodium beef broth,
        Swanson®

3   tablespoons unsalted butter

1. Season short ribs with salt and pepper on all sides. In a large Dutch oven, over medium-high heat, cook short ribs in batches in hot oil until brown on all sides, about 10 minutes per batch. Transfer meat to a platter; keep warm. Set aside.

2. In the same Dutch oven, over high heat, cook the carrots, celery, and garlic for 10 minutes, stirring occasionally. Add the ribs, tomato purée, cognac, red wine, and gravy mix. Cook, uncovered, for 10 minutes or until liquid is slightly reduced. Add broth. Bring to a boil; reduce heat. Simmer, covered, for 2 to 2½ hours or until ribs are tender.

3. Transfer meat and vegetables to a platter, reserving juices in Dutch oven; keep warm. Transfer juices to a small saucepan; skim fat. Bring to a boil; reduce heat. Boil gently, uncovered, about 10 minutes. Stir in butter; heat through. Season with salt and pepper, if necessary.

4. Serve ribs and vegetables in shallow soup bowls with sauce.

Blue Cheese Burger

Prep 15 minutes   **Cook** 12 minutes   **Grill** 10 minutes   **Makes** 4 servings

2	cups Burgundy wine
1	pound lean ground beef
½	cup plain bread crumbs, *Progresso®*
1	large egg
1	teaspoon mesquite seasoning, *McCormick® Grill Mates®*
1	teaspoon coarsely ground pepper, *McCormick®*
8	tablespoons blue cheese, *Sargento®*
1	tablespoon unsalted butter
½	package (8-ounce) sliced mushrooms
1	teaspoon kosher salt
½	teaspoon ground black pepper
	Vegetable oil
4	hamburger buns
	Lettuce
	Sliced tomato
	Sliced red onion

1. In a small saucepan, over high heat, reduce the wine to ½ cup. Remove from heat; cool.

2. In a medium mixing bowl, combine the wine reduction, ground beef, bread crumbs, egg, mesquite seasoning, and coarsely ground black pepper. Mix thoroughly. Form into 8 patties. Place 2 tablespoons of crumbled blue cheese in the center of each of the 4 patties, spreading filling to within ½ inch of the edges. Top with remaining patties, pressing edges together to seal. Wrap with plastic wrap and refrigerate until ready to use.

3. In a medium skillet, over medium-high heat, cook mushrooms in the butter for 6 to 7 minutes or until the mushrooms are browned. Sprinkle with salt and pepper.

4. Meanwhile, set up grill for direct cooking over high heat. Oil grate when ready to start cooking. Place patties on hot oiled grill. Cook for 5 minutes per side for medium (160 degrees F).

5. Serve on toasted buns with mushrooms, lettuce, tomato, and onion.

Salt-Crusted Basil Pork

Prep 20 minutes　　**Bake** 45 minutes　　**Makes** 4 servings

No-stick cooking spray, *Pam®*

2　　pork tenderloins (1 pound each), trimmed

4　　leaves Swiss chard, rinsed and stems removed

¾　　cup pesto sauce, divided use, *Christopher Ranch®*

1　　pound small new potatoes, rinsed and scrubbed

1　　cup fat-free egg whites, *Egg Beaters®*

4　　cups kosher salt

1. Preheat oven to 350 degrees F. Spray the bottom of a 9×13-inch baking pan with cooking spray; set aside.

2. Lay each tenderloin on 2 Swiss chard leaves. Spread each tenderloin with 2 tablespoons of the pesto; wrap with the leaves. Transfer to the center of the baking pan with the ends of the Swiss chard tucked underneath. Place the potatoes around the tenderloins toward the center of the pan. Insert an ovenproof thermometer into one of the tenderloins.

3. In large bowl, whip the egg whites to a stiff peak; fold in the salt to make a paste. Stir in the remaining pesto. Spread the paste over the tenderloins and potatoes, making sure that all are covered. Bake for 4 minutes or until internal temperature reaches 150 degrees F.

4. To serve, remove salt crust from tenderloins by breaking and peeling. Use a fork to fold back the Swiss chard leaves. Transfer tenderloins to platter and slice in ½- to 1-inch slices. Rub most of the salt off potatoes with a paper towel; place potatoes on platter with sliced meat.

NOTE: Substitute 8 real egg whites for the liquid egg whites.

Pork Tenderloin with Mushroom Sauce

Prep 10 minutes   **Bake** 20 minutes   **Stand** 5 minutes   **Cook** 12 minutes   **Makes** 4 servings

1	teaspoon garlic salt, *Lawry's®*
1	teaspoon lemon pepper, *Lawry's®*
1¼	pounds pork tenderloin
2	tablespoons extra virgin olive oil
4	tablespoons butter
½	teaspoon minced garlic, *Gourmet Garden®*
1	package (8-ounce) sliced brown mushrooms
½	cup frozen chopped onions, *Ore-Ida®*
½	cup red wine
1	jar (12-ounce) pork gravy, *Heinz®*

1. Preheat oven to 425 degrees F.

2. In a small bowl, combine garlic salt and lemon pepper. Rub pork tenderloin with seasoning; set aside.

3. In a large ovenproof skillet, over medium-high heat, sear pork on all sides in hot oil. Transfer skillet to the oven. Roast for 20 minutes or until internal temperature reaches 160 degrees F. Let stand for 5 minutes before serving.

4. Meanwhile, in a medium saucepan, over medium-high heat, melt the butter. Add the garlic and mushrooms and cook for 8 to 10 minutes. Add onions, wine, and gravy. Bring to a boil, stirring frequently. Reduce heat and simmer for 3 minutes, stirring occasionally.

5. Serve sliced tenderloin with mushrooms.

Pineapple Ham Loaf

Prep 15 minutes   **Bake** 1½ hours   **Makes** 4 servings

No-stick cooking spray, *Pam*®

FOR THE GLAZE:

½	cup crushed pineapple, *Dole*®
¼	cup brown sugar, *Domino*®/*C&H*®
2	teaspoons stone-ground mustard
1	tablespoon prepared horseradish, *Morehouse*®
¼	cup cider vinegar

FOR THE HAM LOAF:

1	pound smoked ham, coarsely chopped
1	pound lean ground pork
1	tablespoon minced garlic, *Christopher Ranch*®
1	small yellow onion, minced
1	teaspoon kosher salt
1	teaspoon ground black pepper
1	cup crackers, crushed, *Ritz*®
1	egg, beaten
¾	cup 1% milk

1. Preheat oven to 325 degrees F. Spray a 9×5-inch loaf pan with cooking spray; set aside.

2. For the glaze, in a small bowl, stir together the pineapple, brown sugar, mustard, horseradish, and vinegar. Spread about half of the glaze into the bottom of prepared loaf pan. Set aside remaining glaze.

3. For the ham loaf, place ham in a food processor fitted with the steel blade. Pulse briefly, scraping bowl occasionally. Pulse another 3 or 4 times. Do not overprocess or it will turn to paste. Transfer ham to a large mixing bowl; add ground pork, garlic, onion, salt, pepper, crackers, egg, and milk. Stir until combined.

4. Press the ham mixture into the loaf pan; the glaze will rise up the sides. With a sharp knife, make slashes on the top in several places. Bake for 1 hour; brush with the remaining glaze. Bake for another 30 minutes.

Marsala Butter Chicken

Prep 15 minutes   **Cook** 25 minutes   **Makes** 4 servings

4   boneless, skinless chicken breast
       halves

       Salt and ground black pepper

       All-purpose flour

3   tablespoons extra virgin olive oil

12   whole garlic cloves, cut in half,
       Melissa's®

1   bag (16-ounce) peeled baby
       carrots

3   tablespoons unsalted butter

1   cup Marsala wine

1   cup low-sodium chicken broth,
       Swanson®

2   tablespoons sugar, *Domino®/C&H®*

1   teaspoon kosher salt

½   teaspoon coarsely ground black
       pepper

2   teaspoons fresh thyme leaves

1. Place each chicken breast between 2 pieces of plastic wrap. Using the flat side of a meat mallet, pound to ¼ inch thick. Remove plastic. Season with salt and pepper. Place flour in a shallow dish. Coat both sides of chicken in flour; shake off excess. In a large skillet, fry chicken in 2 tablespoons hot oil over medium-high heat for 2 to 3 minutes on each side or until golden. Transfer to a plate; set aside.

2. In the same skillet, over medium-high heat, heat the remaining 1 tablespoon oil. Add the garlic and cook and stir for 2 minutes or until the garlic starts to turn golden brown. Add the carrots and butter; cook and stir for another 2 minutes. Add the wine and the broth. Stir in the sugar, salt, pepper, and thyme. Bring to a boil; reduce heat to medium. Cook for about 10 minutes or until the liquid is reduced by half. Return chicken and juices to the pan, coating with sauce. Simmer for another 5 minutes or until sauce has thickened.

Note: You can substitute 1 teaspoon dried (not ground) thyme leaves for the fresh.

Lemon Turkey Schnitzel

Prep 15 minutes   Cook 10 minutes   Makes 4 servings

FOR THE AÏLOI:

1   cup mayonnaise, *Best Foods® or Hellmann's®*

2   teaspoons crushed garlic, *Gourmet Garden®*

2   tablespoons *Minute Maid® Frozen Lemon Juice,* thawed

1   can diced tomatoes, drained, (15-ounce), *Del Monte®*

FOR THE SCHNITZEL:

4   turkey cutlets (1 pound)

    Sea salt and ground black pepper

2   eggs lightly beaten with 2 tablespoons cold water

1½ cups fine bread crumbs

1   cup canola oil

FOR THE SALAD:

8   cups mixed salad greens, *Fresh Express®*

¼   cup *Newman's Own® Lite Balsamic Dressing*

2   fresh apricots, quartered (or other seasonal fruit [optional])

12 pitted kalamata olives, *Peloponnese®* (optional)

1. Preheat oven to 250 degrees F.

2. For the aïoli, in a small bowl, stir together mayonnaise, garlic, lemon juice, and tomatoes. Cover; refrigerate until ready to serve.

3. For the schnitzel, place each turkey cutlet between 2 pieces of plastic wrap. Using the flat side of a meat mallet, pound to ¼ inch thick. Remove plastic. Season both sides with salt and pepper. Pour egg-water mixture into a shallow dish. Dip turkey into egg mixture to coat. Place the bread crumbs in a second dish. Dip turkey in bread crumbs.

4. In a large skillet, over medium-high heat, heat ½ cup oil. Cook half of the turkey for 3 to 4 minutes on the first side and 2 to 3 minutes on the second side or until golden brown. Transfer to a platter lined with paper towels; keep warm. Remove oil from skillet; carefully wipe skillet with paper towels. Cook remaining turkey in remaining ½ cup hot oil over medium-high heat for 3 to 4 minutes on the first side and 2 to 3 minutes on the second side or until golden brown. Transfer to the platter lined with paper towels; keep warm.

5. For the salad, toss greens with dressing. Serve turkey with salad and aïoli. Garnish with apricots and olives (optional).

Pomegranate-Glazed Duck

Prep 15 minutes   **Marinate** 8 hours   **Cook** 4 minutes   **Bake** 27 minutes   **Stand** 10 minutes   **Makes** 4 servings

FOR THE DUCK BREASTS:

2   cups pomegranate juice, *POM*®

¼   cup honey

2   teaspoons chopped garlic, *Gourmet Garden*®

½   teaspoon pumpkin pie spice, *McCormick*®

1   teaspoon salt

1   teaspoon ground black pepper

4   (5-ounce) skinless, boneless duck breast halves, rinsed and trimmed

1   tablespoon extra virgin olive oil

FOR THE SAUCE:

2   tablespoons red currant jelly

½   cup low-sodium chicken broth, *Swanson*®

2   tablespoons butter, cut into 4 pieces

FOR THE RICE:

No-stick cooking spray, *Pam*®

1   can (15-ounce) cut sweet potatoes, drained, and diced, *Princella*®

2   packages (8.8 ounces each) long grain and wild rice, *Uncle Ben's Ready Rice*®

1   tablespoon unsalted butter

¼   cup real bacon pieces, *Hormel*®

1. For the duck breasts, in a large zip-top plastic bag, combine pomegranate juice, honey, garlic, pumpkin pie spice, salt, and pepper. Squeeze out air and seal. Gently massage bag to combine ingredients. With a sharp knife, score the skin of the duck breasts diagonally. Place breasts in bag. Marinate in the refrigerator overnight. Remove breasts from marinade; reserve marinade.

2. Preheat oven to 450 degrees F. In a medium ovenproof skillet, over medium-high heat, cook breasts in hot oil until lightly browned on both sides, turning once, about 4 minutes. Drain off fat. Transfer pan to the oven. Roast duck for 12 to 15 minutes or until internal temperature reaches 150 degrees F. Transfer duck to a cutting board; keep warm. Let rest 10 minutes.

3. For the sauce, in the same skillet, stir together the jelly, reserved marinade, and chicken broth, one at a time, over high heat. Bring to a boil; reduce heat. Simmer, uncovered, until sauce thickens and coats the back of a spoon, about 10 minutes. Remove from the heat. Strain sauce; return to pan. Stir in butter.

4. For the rice, lightly spray a baking sheet with cooking spray. Arrange potatoes in a single layer on baking sheet. Bake for 15 minutes or until potatoes start to turn slightly brown. Meanwhile, cook rice in microwave according to package directions. Add rice to sweet potatoes; add butter and bacon; stir.

5. Slice duck breasts diagonally across the grain; serve with the sauce and rice. Garnish with *fresh flat-leaf parsley* (optional).

Ale House Salad

Prep 10 minutes **Cook** 14 minutes **Makes** 8 servings

FOR THE BEER DRESSING:

1	tablespoon Italian salad dressing mix, *Good Seasons*®
¼	cup ale-style beer
2	tablespoons malt vinegar, *Heinz*®
1½	teaspoons Dijon mustard, *Grey Poupon*®
3	tablespoons olive oil

FOR THE SALAD:

2	bags (16 ounces each) seasoned diced potatoes, *Reser's*®
1	bag (12-ounce) frozen haricots verts, thawed, *C&W*®
1½	cups cherry tomatoes, cut in half
¼	cup real crumbled bacon, *Hormel*®

1. For the beer dressing, in a screw-top jar, add salad dressing mix, beer, vinegar, mustard, and oil. Cover and shake well; set aside.

2. For the salad, add potatoes to a microwave-safe bowl; cover and cook on high setting (100 percent power) for 8 to 10 minutes. Set aside. Add haricots verts to a microwave-safe bowl with 1 tablespoon water. Cover and cook on high setting (100 percent power) for 6 to 8 minutes or until crisp-tender. Drain.

3. In a large bowl, combine potatoes, haricots verts, tomatoes, and bacon. Toss with dressing and serve.

Stewed Butter Beans and Ham

Prep 5 minutes **Cook** 30 minutes **Makes** 4 servings

1	package (6-ounce) ham steak, cut into bite-size pieces, *Farmer John*®
2	cans (15 ounces each) butter beans, rinsed and drained, *Seaside*®
1	cup frozen chopped onions, *Ore-Ida*®
1	teaspoon kosher salt
¼	teaspoon ground black pepper
1	bay leaf, *McCormick*®

1. In a medium saucepan, combine the ham, butter beans, onions, salt, pepper, and bay leaf in enough water to barely cover. Bring to a boil; reduce heat to medium-high heat. Cook, covered, for 30 to 45 minutes or until most of the water has evaporated.

Cheesy Stuffed Potatoes

Prep 20 minutes   **Cook** 8 minutes   **Bake** 15 minutes   **Broil** 2 minutes   **Makes** 4 potato halves

2	microwave russet potatoes, *Micro Baker®*
2	tablespoons butter
⅓	cup heavy cream
1	teaspoon salad supreme seasoning, *McCormick®*
1	teaspoon parsley flakes, *McCormick®*
	Salt and ground black pepper
1	jar (4.5-ounce) sliced mushrooms, drained, *Green Giant®*
½	cup Gouda cheese, cut into 1-inch cubes
	Chopped scallions (optional)

1. Preheat oven to 400 degrees F. Line a baking sheet with foil; set aside.

2. Microwave potatoes, in wrapper, on high setting (100 percent power) for 8 to 10 minutes. Remove; let stand 5 minutes. Remove wrappers and cut potatoes in half lengthwise. Scoop pulp out of potatoes and place in a large bowl. Place skins on baking sheet; set aside. Mash the potato pulp, butter, cream, salad seasoning, and parsley with a potato masher. Season with salt and pepper. Stir in mushrooms and Gouda. Divide mashed potato mixture evenly among the potato shells.

3. Bake for 15 to 17 minutes or until centers are hot and cheese is melted. Preheat broiler. Broil potatoes, 6 inches from heat source, for 2 to 3 minutes or until tops are browned. Sprinkle with chopped scallions (optional).

Brie Hash Brown Casserole

Prep 10 minutes   **Cook** 6 minutes   **Bake** 35 minutes   **Makes** 8 servings

	No-stick cooking spray, *Pam®*
2	tablespoons butter
1	package (8-ounce) sliced mushrooms
1	can condensed cream of mushroom soup, *Campbell's®*
½	cup melted butter
1½	teaspoons kosher salt
½	teaspoon ground black pepper
1	cup yellow onion, chopped
2	containers (5 ounces each) brie cheese, rind removed, chopped, *Alouette Creme de Brie®*
1	bag (30-ounce) country-style hash browns, thawed, *Ore-Ida®*

1. Preheat oven to 350 degrees F. Spray 9×13-inch baking pan with cooking spray; set aside.

2. In a medium skillet, over medium-high heat, melt butter. Add mushrooms and cook 6 to 8 minutes or until tender. Transfer to a large bowl. Add soup, butter, salt, pepper, onions, and Brie cheese; mix well. Add hash browns; pour into baking pan. Bake for 35 minutes, or until golden brown and cheese has melted. If top has not browned after 40 minutes, turn broiler to high and cook until top is brown, about 3 to 4 minutes.

Asian American

The next time you're craving the zesty flavors of Asian cooking—ginger, garlic, chiles, soy, and sesame—skip the takeout. These recipes are inspired by my favorite Thai, Chinese, and Japanese restaurant dishes but are simple enough to stir up in your own kitchen.

Sesame Steak Stir Fry

Prep 10 minutes   **Marinate** 8 to 24 hours   **Cook** 17 minutes   **Makes** 4 servings

2   pounds flank or skirt steak

¾   cup sesame salad dressing, *Annie's Naturals® Asian Sesame Organic*

2   tablespoons light soy sauce, *Kikkoman®*

2   tablespoons lemon juice, *Minute Maid®*

2   tablespoons minced ginger, *Gourmet Garden®*

4   teaspoons crushed garlic, divided, *Gourmet Garden®*

2   tablespoons canola oil

1   large yellow onion, chopped

2   bunches Swiss chard, leaves separated, rinsed, patted dry, and coarsely chopped

1   teaspoon toasted sesame oil, *Dynasty®*

1. Slice steak into ½-inch strips, slicing against the grain.

2. Place steak in a large zip-top plastic bag and add the salad dressing, soy sauce, lemon juice, ginger, and 1 teaspoon garlic. Squeeze out air and seal. Gently massage bag to combine ingredients. Marinate in refrigerator for 8 to 24 hours. Remove steaks from the marinade; reserve marinade.

3. In a large skillet or wok, over high heat, heat 1 tablespoon of the oil. Add beef and stir-fry for 5 minutes. Remove from skillet.

4. Add the remaining 1 tablespoon oil to pan. Add onion and remaining 3 teaspoons garlic; stir-fry for 3 minutes. Add chard and stir-fry for another 3 minutes. Add ½ cup *water* and stir-fry until almost dry. Add the reserved marinade, another ¼ cup *water*, and stir-fry until almost dry. Add steak to pan and stir-fry for 2 minutes or until heated through. Drizzle with sesame oil just before serving.

Cider Ginger Beef

Prep 15 minutes   **Marinate** 30 minutes   **Cook** 5 minutes   **Makes** 4 servings

FOR THE BEEF:

1½   **pounds flank or skirt steak**

3   **tablespoons stir-fry sauce,** *Kikkoman*®

3   **tablespoons dry sherry,** *Christian Brothers*®

1   **tablespoon sugar,** *Domino*®/*C&H*®

1   **tablespoon minced ginger,** *Gourmet Garden*®

FOR THE STIR-FRY:

8   **whole heads baby bok choy, cut in half lengthwise**

2   **tablespoons stir-fry sauce,** *Kikkoman*®

3   **tablespoons dry sherry,** *Christian Brothers*®

1   **teaspoon rice vinegar or cider vinegar**

3   **tablespoons peanut oil**

1½   **tablespoons crushed garlic,** *Gourmet Garden*®

1   **tablespoon minced ginger,** *Gourmet Garden*®

¼   **cup ginger preserves,** *Robertson's*®

1   **teaspoon toasted sesame oil,** *Dynasty*®

    Hot white rice

1. For the beef, slice steak across the grain into ¼-inch-thick slices; cut slices into 2- to 3-inch strips.

2. In a large zip-top bag, combine stir-fry sauce, sherry, sugar, and ginger. Squeeze out air and seal. Gently massage bag to dissolve sugar. Add steak. Gently massage bag to combine ingredients. Marinate in the refrigerator for 30 minutes to 1 hour.

3. For the stir-fry, bring a large pot of water to a boil; add the bok choy. Blanch for 1 minute; drain immediately and rinse with cold water. Drain on paper towels.

4. In a small bowl, stir together stir-fry sauce, sherry, and vinegar; set aside. Remove steak from marinade; discard marinade.

5. In a large skillet or wok, over high heat, heat peanut oil. Add garlic and ginger and stir-fry 30 seconds. Add beef and stir-fry for 3 minutes. Add the sauce mixture and bok choy; stir-fry until mixture is just heated through, about 1 minute. Stir in ginger preserves. Drizzle with sesame oil and serve with rice.

Wasabi Plum Pork Chops

Prep 15 minutes   **Cook** 12 minutes   **Bake** 14 minutes   **Makes** 4 servings

No-stick cooking spray, *Pam*®

FOR THE SAUCE:

1	**can (15-ounce) purple plums with syrup, pitted and quartered (reserve ½ cup juice),** *Oregon*®
¼	**cup hoisin sauce,** *Lee Kum Kee*®
½	**cup dried apricots, slivered,** *Sun-Maid*®
2	**teaspoons crushed garlic,** *Gourmet Garden*®
2	**star anise pods**
1	**teaspoon wasabi paste**
1	**cup light coconut milk,** *Thai House*®

FOR THE CHOPS:

4	**boneless, pork loin chops (6 to 8 ounces each)**
½	**teaspoon salt**
2	**tablespoons minced ginger,** *Gourmet Garden*®
1	**tablespoon crushed garlic,** *Gourmet Garden*®

FOR THE SLAW:

1	**bag (12-ounce) broccoli coleslaw,** *Mann's*®
¼	**cup hoisin sauce,** *Lee Kum Kee*®
¾	**cup wasabi peas**

1. Preheat oven to 425 degrees F. Spray a rimmed baking sheet with cooking spray; heat sheet for 6 to 8 minutes.

2. Meanwhile, for the sauce, in a medium saucepan, stir together the plums, reserved ½ cup plum juice, hoisin sauce, apricots, garlic, and star anise. Bring to a boil; reduce heat. Simmer, uncovered, until apricots are plump, about 10 to 15 minutes. Remove star anise and stir in wasabi and coconut milk. Keep warm.

3. For the pork chops, rub with the salt, ginger, and garlic. Spray chops with cooking spray on both sides and place on the hot baking sheet. Bake for 6 minutes and turn the chops over. Bake for 8 minutes more or until chops are browned and internal temperature reaches 150 degrees F. Keep warm.

4. For the slaw, in a large bowl, toss the broccoli coleslaw and hoisin sauce.

5. Serve chops with sauce and slaw sprinkled with wasabi peas.

Coconut Curried Pork

Prep 15 minutes   **Marinate** 1 hour   **Cook** 5 hours (Low)   **Makes** 4 servings

6	center-cut loin pork chops (4 ounces each)
½	teaspoon salt
½	teaspoon ground black pepper
¼	cup lime juice, *ReaLime®*
1	tablespoon grated ginger, *Gourmet Garden®*
1	cup chopped onion, *Ore Ida®*
1	tablespoon red curry paste, *Thai House®*
½	cup low-sodium chicken broth, *Swanson®*
1	can (14 ounce) light coconut milk, *Thai House®*
½	cup chopped dried apricots, *Sun-Maid®*
2	tablespoons honey, *Sue Bee®*
1	tablespoon chopped garlic, *Gourmet Garden®*
½	tablespoon cornstarch
	Cooked white rice
¼	cup thinly sliced scallions (optional)

1. Place pork chops in a large zip-top plastic bag and add the salt, pepper, lime juice, and ginger. Squeeze air out of bag and seal. Gently massage bag to combine ingredients. Marinate in the refrigerator for 1 to 24 hours.

2. In a large saucepan, over medium-high heat, mix onion, curry paste, chicken broth, coconut milk, apricots, honey, and garlic; bring to a boil. Place pork chops in a 4-quart slow cooker; add the mixture from the saucepan.

3. Cook over Low heat for 5 to 6 hours.

4. Remove pork chops from sauce; place on platter. Pour sauce into a saucepan; bring to a boil. Combine cornstarch and ½ tablespoon *water;* add to boiling sauce. Simmer for 2 to 3 minutes.

5. Serve in shallow soup bowls with rice, ladling extra sauce over the chops. Sprinkle with sliced scallions (optional).

Cashew-Orange Chicken

Prep 20 minutes   **Marinate** 8 hours   **Cook** 4 minutes   **Makes** 4 servings

FOR THE MARINADE:

1	tablespoon minced ginger, *Gourmet Garden*®
1	tablespoon crushed garlic, *Gourmet Garden*®
1	bottle (11.75-ounce) stir-fry sauce, *Kikkoman*®
2	tablespoons orange juice concentrate, *Minute Maid*®
⅓	cup thinly sliced green onions
6	small dried hot red chile peppers, (optional)
2	pounds boneless, skinless chicken breasts, cut diagonally into ½-inch pieces

FOR THE STIR-FRY:

¼	cup peanut oil
1	cup cashew halves
1	tablespoon orange marmalade, *Hero*®
1	tablespoon toasted sesame oil

1. For the marinade, place ginger, garlic, stir-fry sauce, orange juice concentrate, green onions, and chiles (optional) in a large zip-top bag. Squeeze out air and seal. Gently massage bag to combine ingredients. Add chicken. Marinate in the refrigerator 8 to 24 hours. When ready to cook, remove chicken, reserving marinade; set aside.

2. For the stir-fry, over high heat, in a large skillet or wok, heat oil. Add chicken and stir-fry for 2 to 3 minutes or until almost cooked through. Drain off extra oil.

3. Add the reserved marinade, cashews, and orange marmalade; stir-fry for an additional 2 minutes or until heated through. Drizzle with sesame oil just before serving.

Mustard-Crusted Chicken

Prep 5 minutes   **Cook** 8 minutes   **Bake** 17 minutes   **Makes** 4 servings

No-stick cooking spray, *Pam®*

FOR THE CHICKEN:

3	tablespoons unsalted butter
1	tablespoon chopped garlic, *Gourmet Garden®*
1	tablespoon minced ginger, *Gourmet Garden®*
½	cup panko crumbs
	Salt and ground black pepper
1	tablespoon Dijon mustard, *Grey Poupon®*
2	tablespoons lime juice, *ReaLime®*
4	boneless, skinless chicken breasts
1	lime, cut into wedges (optional)

FOR THE VEGETABLES:

1	package (16-ounce) frozen stir-fry vegetables with teriyaki sauce, *Green Giant®*
1	tablespoon minced ginger, *Gourmet Garden®*

1. For the chicken, preheat oven to 450 degrees F. Spray a rimmed baking sheet with cooking spray.

2. In a small skillet, over medium-high heat, melt butter. Add garlic and ginger; cook and stir for 2 to 3 minutes. Add panko crumbs and mix well. Remove from heat and spread on plate to cool. Season with salt and pepper.

3. In a small bowl, stir the mustard and lime juice until smooth. Brush onto chicken breasts; press crumb mixture evenly over top. Place breasts on a rimmed baking sheet; spray with cooking spray. Bake for 12 to 15 minutes or until internal temperature reaches 170 degrees F and crumbs are golden brown.

4. For the vegetables, in a large skillet, over medium-high heat, cook vegetables, contents of sauce packet, and ginger for 4 to 5 minutes, stirring occasionally, until heated through.

5. Serve chicken with vegetables. Garnish with lime wedges (optional).

Tokyo Chicken Salad

Prep 30 minutes   **Cook** 20 minutes   **Makes** 6 servings

3	pounds russet potatoes, skin on, cut in 1 inch cubes
3	medium pickling cucumbers, very thinly sliced (about ¾ cup)
1	teaspoon kosher salt
1	cup Italian dressing, *Newman's Own*®
2	tablespoons seasoned rice wine vinegar, *Marukan*®
2	cups rotisserie chicken, white meat only, shredded
½	head iceberg lettuce, shredded
1	medium red onion, thinly sliced, soaked in cold water, drained
4	roma tomatoes, thinly sliced
1	bunch red radishes, thinly sliced
1	medium carrot, peeled and thinly sliced into coins
1	cup mayonnaise, *Best Foods*® or *Hellmann's*®
	Kosher salt and cracked black pepper

1. In a large stockpot, place potatoes and enough salted water to cover. Bring to a boil; reduce the heat. Simmer, covered, for 20 to 25 minutes or just until tender. Drain well; cool slightly. Place cooked potatoes in a large mixing bowl. Mash lightly with a potato masher or a ricer, leaving half of them cubed and half of them mashed.

2. Meanwhile, in a small bowl, toss cucumber with the kosher salt. After 10 to 15 minutes, rinse cucumbers; drain and blot dry with paper towels. Set aside.

3. Pour the Italian dressing and vinegar over the potatoes while still warm. Add the cucumbers, chicken, lettuce, onion, tomatoes, radishes, and carrots. Add mayonnaise. Toss lightly to coat. Season to taste with salt and pepper.

Note: This salad is best eaten the day it is made.

Miso Jasmine Cod

Prep 10 minutes   **Marinate** 8 hours   **Stand** 20 minutes   **Broil** 6 minutes   **Cook** 25 minutes   **Makes** 4 servings

FOR THE COD:

¼	cup white wine
1	packet (1.05-ounce) miso soup mix, *Kikkoman*®
3	tablespoons sugar, *Domino*®/*C&H*®
2	pounds black cod fillets
	No-stick cooking spray, *Pam*®
8	blades chives (optional)

FOR THE RICE:

1	cup jasmine rice, rinsed
2	cups vegetable broth, *Swanson*®

FOR THE SPINACH:

1	package (10-ounce) fresh baby spinach, *Dole*®
2	tablespoons extra virgin olive oil
½	cup frozen chopped yellow onions, *Ore-Ida*®
1	teaspoon kosher salt

1. For the cod, place wine, miso soup mix, and sugar in a large zip-top bag; set aside. Squeeze out air and seal. Massage gently to combine ingredients. Rinse the fish with cold water and dry thoroughly with paper towels. Place the fish in the bag. Marinate in refrigerator 8 to 24 hours. Let marinated fish sit at room temperature for 20 to 30 minutes. Remove fillets from bag; discard marinade.

2. For the rice, in a medium saucepan, combine rice and broth. Bring to a boil; reduce heat. Simmer, covered, for 20 minutes.

3. Preheat broiler. Place fish on a foil-lined baking sheet or broiler pan sprayed with cooking spray. Broil 3 to 5 minutes per side or until fish easily flakes with a fork and is well caramelized.

4. For the spinach, clean spinach and drain. Heat a large saucepan or skillet over medium-high heat; add olive oil and onion. Cook and stir for 3 minutes or until the onion turns opaque; do not brown the onion. Add wet spinach. As the spinach starts to cook down, add the salt. Stir the spinach until it is completely wilted.

5. Serve the fish with the rice and spinach. Sprinkle with chives (optional).

Minty Cucumber Salad

Prep 15 minutes   Chill 1 hour   Makes 4 servings

6	small pickling cucumbers
1½	teaspoons kosher salt
¼	cup chopped dry-roasted peanuts, *Planters®*
3	tablespoons unseasoned rice vinegar, *Nakano®*
1	tablespoon water
1	tablespoon sugar, *Domino®/C&H®*
12	leaves fresh mint, each torn into fourths
2	tablespoons chopped fresh cilantro
2	teaspoons chili sauce, *Lee Kum Kee®*

1. Rinse the cucumbers and pat dry with paper towels. Slice them lengthwise no more than ⅛ inch thick. Toss with the salt.

2. In a medium bowl, stir together the peanuts, rice vinegar, water, sugar, mint, cilantro, and chili sauce. When the sugar is dissolved, add the cucumbers and toss to cover. Cover with plastic wrap; chill 1 hour before serving and up to 1 week.

Chile-Garlic Pancakes

Start to Finish 20 minutes   **Makes** 6 servings

1   bag cut sweet potatoes, *Ore-Ida®
     Steam 'n Mash™*

1   tablespoon minced ginger,
     Gourmet Garden®

1   tablespoon chile-garlic sauce,
     Lee Kum Kee®

3   eggs, lightly beaten

¾   cup light coconut milk, *Thai
     Kitchen®*

½   cup all-purpose flour

1   teaspoon salt

¼   teaspoon ground white pepper

¼   cup thinly sliced scallions, plus
     more for garnish

2   tablespoons finely chopped
     fresh cilantro

     Canola oil

1. Microwave sweet potatoes according to package directions. Mash the sweet potatoes; set aside.

2. In a large bowl, stir together ginger, chile-garlic sauce, beaten eggs, coconut milk, flour, salt, white pepper, scallions, and cilantro. Fold in mashed sweet potatoes until just combined.

3. In a large skillet, over medium-high heat, heat ⅛-inch oil. Spoon batter into skillet; fry until golden brown on both sides. Garnish with scallions.

Coast to Coast

Fish is light, fresh, and flavorful—and the news coming in from the health front is that we're supposed to be eating a lot more of it. Adding more fish to my diet inspired me to come up with interesting ways to cook it that go beyond broiling it with butter and lemon. Here are some delicicous ways you can add more fish to your diet too.

Revved-Up Tilapia

Prep 5 minutes   Cook 25 minutes   Makes 4 servings

2   tablespoons unsalted butter

1   tablespoon minced garlic,
       Gourmet Garden®

½   cup yellow onion, diced

1½   cups converted rice, *Uncle Ben's*®

2½   cups chicken broth, *Swanson's*®

1   can (10-ounce) chopped tomatoes
       with green chiles, *Ro-Tel*®

1½   teaspoons smoky sweet pepper
       seasoning, *McCormick*®

1½   pounds tilapia fillets

¼   teaspoon kosher salt

¼   cup finely chopped fresh cilantro
       or parsley

1. In a large skillet, over medium-high heat, melt butter. Add garlic and onion; cook and stir for 1 to 2 minutes or until softened. Add the rice. Cook and stir for about 5 minutes or until rice is a golden brown color. Increase heat to high; add broth, tomatoes, and ½ teaspoon pepper seasoning. Bring to a boil and reduce heat. Simmer, covered, for another 5 minutes.

2. Season tilapia with salt and remaining 1 teaspoon pepper seasoning. Place fish in skillet on top of the rice. Cover and simmer for another 12 to 15 minutes or until the fish is opaque. Remove from heat. Sprinkle with cilantro.

Hawaiian Luau Sea Bass

Prep 10 minutes   **Marinate** 2 hours   **Cook** 15 minutes   **Makes** 4 servings

4   (6-ounce) sea bass fillets

Kosher salt and ground black pepper

1   cup pineapple juice, *Dole®*

1   cup mandarin oranges, *Del Monte® SunFresh®*

1   cup Hawaiian-style fruit medley, *Del Monte® SunFresh®*

1   tablespoon fresh thyme leaves

¼   teaspoon cayenne pepper

No-stick cooking spray, *Pam®*

2   scallions, white part only, cut into julienne strips (optional)

1. Rinse the fillets and pat dry with paper towels. Season with salt and pepper.

2. In a large zip-top plastic bag, place the pineapple juice, mandarin oranges, fruit medley, thyme, and cayenne pepper. Squeeze out air and seal. Gently massage bag to combine ingredients. Add fish and turn to coat. Marinate in the refrigerator for 2 to 4 hours, turning the bag occasionally. Remove fish and fruit from marinade; reserve marinade.

3. Spray a steamer rack with cooking spray. Place steamer in a large skillet. Add reserved marinade to the skillet; add water to marinade if necessary. Arrange fish on rack. Bring marinade to a boil; cover and steam fish for 8 minutes or until just opaque in the center. Transfer fish to plates; keep warm. Remove rack from skillet and add the fruit to the liquid in the skillet. Boil about 6 minutes or until reduced enough to coat a spoon. To serve, spoon sauce over fish. Garnish with scallions (optional).

Balsamic Seared Ahi
with Gorgonzola Salad

Prep 10 minutes   **Chill** 2 hours   **Cook** 2 minutes   **Makes** 4 servings

1	cup red or black seedless grapes, cut in half
½	cup balsamic vinegar, *Pompeian®*
3	ounces Gorgonzola, crumbled, *Stella®*
4	(6-ounce) ahi tuna steaks
1	tablespoon, plus ¼ cup extra virgin olive oil, *Pompeian®*
8	cups romaine lettuce mix, *Fresh Express®*
1	teaspoon kosher salt

1. Place the grapes in a shallow dish and add the vinegar. Cover with plastic wrap. Refrigerate for 1 hour. Remove grapes from the vinegar; reserve vinegar in the dish. Place the grapes in a medium salad bowl. Add cheese and toss to coat. Refrigerate until ready to use.

2. Add tuna to the vinegar. Cover with plastic wrap and chill for 1 hour. Remove fish from vinegar and pat dry with paper towels. In a nonstick skillet, sear fish in hot oil for 1 to 3 minutes per side.

3. Add lettuce, remaining ¾ cup oil, and salt to grapes. Serve sliced seared ahi over grape and Gorgonzola salad.

Rosa-Sauced Seafood Loaf

Prep 15 minutes   **Cook** 2 minutes   **Bake** 45 minutes   **Stand** 10 minutes   **Makes** 6 servings

No-stick cooking spray, *Pam*®

FOR THE SEAFOOD LOAF:

8	ounces cooked salmon fillet
1	package (10-ounce) lump crabmeat, *Blue Star*®
3	cans (4 ounces each) tiny shrimp, drained, *Chicken of the Sea*®
⅓	cup unsalted butter, melted
2	cups low-fat milk, hot
2¼	cups crushed saltines (about 65 crackers)
2	teaspoons lemon pepper seasoning, *Lawry's*®
	Kosher salt and ground black pepper
4	large eggs, well beaten
1	lemon, cut into wedges (optional)
	Fresh basil (optional)

FOR THE SAUCE:

1	packet (1.3-ounce) parma rosa sauce mix, *Knorr*®
1½	cups low-fat milk
¼	cup fresh basil (chop all except 1 tablespoon)

1. Preheat oven to 350 degrees F. Spray 9×5-inch loaf pan with cooking spray; set aside.

2. For the seafood loaf, remove skin and bones from the salmon and place in a large bowl. Add the crab and shrimp and mash together until it's a fine mixture. Add the butter, milk, saltines, and lemon pepper and mix well. Season with salt and pepper. Add the eggs and mix well. Place fish mixture in prepared loaf pan. Place the loaf pan in a 9×13-inch pan filled with 1 inch of hot water. Bake for 45 to 50 minutes or until thermometer reads 160 degrees F. Turn loaf out onto a platter; let rest for 10 minutes.

3. For the sauce, in a small saucepan, combine the sauce mix and milk. Bring to a boil; reduce heat. Simmer 2 minutes or until thickened. Stir in chopped basil. Pour a little of the sauce on top of the loaf. Garnish with lemon wedges (optional) and remaining basil (optional). Serve remaining sauce on the side.

Spicy Crab Cakes
with Mango-Avocado Salsa

Prep 20 minutes   Chill 1 hour   Cook 8 minutes   Makes 4 servings

FOR THE CRAB CAKES:

½	cup mayonnaise, *Best Foods® or Hellmann's®*
¼	cup coarse-grain mustard, *Inglehoffer®*
2	teaspoons crab seasoning, *Old Bay®*
1	teaspoon ground black pepper
¾	teaspoon celery seeds, crushed
1	pound jumbo lump crabmeat
¼	cup finely chopped fresh parsley
¼	cup thinly sliced scallions
2	tablespoons canned jalapeño pepper, finely chopped
2	cups finely crushed saltine crackers (about 56 crackers)
2	tablespoons unsalted butter
2	tablespoons olive oil

FOR THE SALSA:

1	cup mango habañero salsa, *Mrs. Renfro's®*
2	avocados, peeled, pitted, chopped and drizzled with lemon juice

1. For the crab cakes, in a small bowl, combine the mayonnaise, mustard, crab seasoning, black pepper, and celery seeds; set aside. Drain crabmeat; gently squeeze to remove excess liquid. In a large mixing bowl, combine crabmeat, parsley, scallion, and jalapeño pepper, breaking up the lumps of crabmeat. Fold in mayonnaise mixture and 1½ cups of the crackers until blended. Form crab mixture into 4 patties, 3 to 4 inches in diameter and 1½ inches thick. Dip into reserved crackers to coat all sides. Place patties on a plate; cover and chill for 1 to 2 hours.

2. In a large skillet, over medium-high heat, heat butter and oil. Cook crab cakes for 4 to 5 minutes on each side until golden, carefully turning once.

3. For the salsa, combine the salsa and three-fourths of the chopped avocado. Serve crab cakes with the salsa. Garnish with the reserved avocado (optional).

Butter Beer Steamers

Prep 5 minutes   Cook 15 minutes   Makes 4 servings

½   cup butter

1   container (5-ounce) diced onions,
     Ready Pac®

2   tablespoons chopped garlic,
     Gourmet Garden®

3   bottles (12-ounce) dark beer, *Bass®*

1   cup water

½   teaspoon red pepper flakes,
     McCormick®

1   teaspoon kosher salt

4   pounds clams, cleaned and
     scrubbed

3   tablespoons finely chopped fresh
     parsley

1   cup butter, melted

     Crusty loaf of bread

1. In a large pot, over medium-high heat, melt butter. Add onions and garlic and cook and stir until soft. Add beer, water, red pepper flakes, and salt. Bring to a boil. Add clams and reduce heat to low. Steam clams for 5 to 10 minutes or until shells have opened. Discard clams that did not open. Divide clams and broth among four bowls. Sprinkle with parsley. Serve with melted butter and bread.

Maine Hottie Dogs

Prep 15 minutes   Chill 30 minutes   Cook 4 minutes   Makes 2 servings

Salt

¾ cup diced cucumber, peeled and seeded

8 ounces fully cooked lobster tail or meat

¼ cup olive oil mayonnaise, *Best Foods® or Hellmann's®*

1 scallion, thinly sliced

1 teaspoon fresh tarragon

1 teaspoon lemon juice, *Minute Maid®*

½ teaspoon Italian dressing mix, *Good Seasons®*

Ground black pepper

Butter

2 hot dog buns or sandwich rolls

1. Lightly salt the cucumber; wrap in paper towels and allow the water to drain for about 10 minutes. Pat dry with fresh paper towels.

2. In a medium bowl, combine the cucumber, lobster, mayonnaise, scallion, tarragon, lemon juice, and dressing mix. Season with pepper. Cover with plastic wrap; chill for 30 minutes to 1 hour.

3. Lightly butter both sides of the buns. In a large heavy skillet, lightly toast the buns for 2 minutes on each side or until golden brown. Spoon the chilled lobster salad onto the warm buns.

Crispy Coconut Shrimp

Prep 15 minutes **Stand** 10 minutes **Bake** 12 minutes **Makes** 4 servings

	No-stick cooking spray, *Pam*®
1	**cup all-purpose flour**
2	**tablespoons powdered sugar,** *Domino*®/*C&H*®
1	**teaspoon paprika,** *McCormick*®
⅓	**cup egg substitute,** *Egg Beaters*®
¼	**cup milk**
1	**teaspoon kosher salt**
2	**cups shredded coconut**
1	**pound large shrimp (16 to 21 count), peeled and deveined**

1. Preheat oven to 425 degrees F. Spray a rimmed baking sheet with cooking spray; set aside.

2. In a shallow bowl, combine flour, powdered sugar, and paprika. In a second bowl, beat together the egg, milk, and salt. Place the coconut in a third bowl. Dip the shrimp in egg wash, then flour mixture, then back in the egg wash, and dredge in the coconut. Let rest for 10 minutes. Place shrimp 2 inches apart on the prepared baking sheet. Bake for 12 to 15 minutes or until golden brown and crisp.

Creamy Shrimp Fettuccine

Prep 10 minutes   **Cook** 15 minutes   **Makes** 4 servings

2   tablespoons extra virgin olive oil

1   large yellow onion, thinly sliced lengthwise

2   cups shredded fresh carrots

1   tablespoon chopped garlic, *Gourmet Garden*®

1½   pounds medium shrimp (26 to 30 count)

1   cup dry white wine

1½   cups half-and-half

1   packet (1.6-ounce) garlic and herb sauce mix, *Knorr*®

½   cup minced fresh parsley

Kosher salt and ground black pepper

1   package (16-ounce) fettuccine, prepared according to package directions

1. In a large skillet, over medium-high heat, heat the oil. Add the onion, carrots, and garlic; cook and stir for 5 minutes or until onion is translucent and carrots are crisp-tender. Add the shrimp and cook and stir for 3 minutes more. Add the wine and reduce the liquid by half. In a small bowl, combine the half-and-half and sauce mix. Add to the onion mixture; bring to a boil, stirring frequently. Add the parsley and simmer for 2 minutes or until the sauce is thickened, stirring occasionally. Season to taste with salt and pepper. Toss sauce with the pasta.

Lemon Alfredo Pasta

Prep 5 minutes   **Cook** 12 minutes   **Makes** 4 servings

1	medium yellow onion, finely chopped
1	tablespoon extra virgin olive oil
1	bag (10-ounce) sweet peas, *Cascadian Farm*®
5	slices prosciutto, chopped
1	packet (1.6-ounce) **Alfredo sauce mix,** *Knorr*®
1½	cups milk
½	cup cream
1	lemon, zested and finely chopped
½	cup shredded **Parmigiano-Reggiano cheese**
1	box (16-ounce) fettuccine, cooked according to package directions
¼	cup finely chopped fresh flat-leaf parsley

1. In a large skillet, over medium-high heat, cook and stir onion in hot oil for 5 minutes or until translucent. Add peas and prosciutto and cook for 5 more minutes.

2. In a small bowl, combine the sauce mix, milk, and cream; mix well. Add to skillet. Bring to a boil; simmer for 2 minutes or until the sauce thickens, stirring constantly. Add the lemon zest and cheese. Toss sauce with the cooked pasta. Sprinkle each serving with parsley.

Summer Squash Bake

Prep 10 minutes   **Cook** 10 minutes   **Bake** 20 minutes   **Makes** 4 servings

No-stick cooking spray, *Pam*®

3   tablespoons unsalted butter

1   medium yellow onion, chopped

1   tablespoon minced garlic, *Gourmet Garden*®

1   bag (16-ounce) chopped frozen yellow crookneck squash, thawed, *Pictsweet*®

¾   cup light sour cream

1   teaspoon sugar, *Domino*®/*C&H*®

1   cup grated cheddar cheese, *Sargento*®

1   cup saltine crackers (about 28 crackers), crushed, *Nabisco*®

Kosher salt and pepper

1. Preheat oven to 350 degrees F. Spray an 8×8-inch baking dish with cooking spray; set aside.

2. In a medium skillet, over medium-high heat, melt butter. Add onions and garlic; cook and stir for 7 minutes or until golden brown. Reduce heat; add squash and cook and stir for 2 more minutes or until squash is tender. Stir in the sour cream, sugar, ¾ cup cheese, and crackers. Season with salt and pepper. Pour into the prepared baking dish; sprinkle with the remaining ¼ cup cheese. Bake for 20 minutes or until the cheese is melted and the top is light golden brown.

Desserts

Who says something special and sweet can't be a weeknight treat? My introduction to the world of cooking was baking cakes with my grandmother. I still like to bake as often as I can. The recipes for these cakes, tarts, pastries, cookies, candies, and cobblers use smart shortcuts to make a homemade dessert an anytime proposition.

How to Make Colored Sugar

Making your own colored sugar is inexpensive, easy, and fast. When you make your own, any color is possible, and any color can be as dark or as light as you like.
1. Place ½ cup sugar in a zip-top bag or glass container with a tight-fitting lid. Add 3 drops of food coloring to the bag or jar.
2. Shake the bag continuously to mix until the color is evenly distributed throughout and the sugar is a uniform color. Pour sugar onto a clean baking sheet and let it air dry for an hour or two.
3. When it's dry, store in a plastic bag or a glass jar or salt shaker.

Sweet Potato Cake
with Citrus Glaze

Prep 15 minutes   **Bake** 45 minutes   **Cool** 10 minutes   **Makes** 10 servings

Butter-flavored cooking spray, *Pam®*

FOR THE CAKE:

1	box (18.25-ounce) spice cake mix, *Betty Crocker®*
2	cups mashed sweet potatoes, *Princella®*
3	eggs
1	teaspoon orange extract, *McCormick®*
1 ¼	cups evaporated milk, *Carnation®*
¼	cup vegetable oil

FOR THE GLAZE:

2	cups powdered sugar, sifted, *Domino®/C&H®*
1	cup lemon curd, stirred, *Dickinson's®*
¼	cup no-pulp orange juice, *Minute Maid®*
3	tablespoons orange liqueur, *Grand Mariner®*
½	teaspoon pumpkin pie spice, *McCormick®*

Red food coloring, *McCormick®*

Yellow food coloring, *McCormick®*

1. Preheat oven to 350 F degrees. Lightly spray a 9-inch fluted cake pan with cooking spray; set aside.

2. For cake, in a large mixing bowl, combine cake mix, sweet potatoes, eggs, orange extract, evaporated milk, and oil; beat with an electric mixer on low speed for 30 seconds. Scrape down sides of bowl; beat for 2 minutes on medium speed. Pour batter into prepared pan. Bake in preheated oven for 45 to 55 minutes or until a toothpick inserted in center comes out clean. Cool on wire rack for 10 minutes. Invert cake from pan and cool completely on wire rack.

3. For glaze, in a medium saucepan, over low heat, cook and stir powdered sugar, lemon curd, orange juice, orange liqueur, and pumpkin pie spice for 10 minutes. If glaze seems too dry, add more orange juice until glaze reaches drizzling consistency.

4. In a small bowl, combine 2 parts yellow food coloring with 4 parts red food coloring and stir to make orange food coloring. Stir into glaze. Drizzle glaze over the cake.

Mardi Gras King Cake

Prep 15 minutes   Bake 16 minutes   Makes 16 servings

2   cans (13.9 ounces each)
    refrigerated orange sweet rolls,
    Pillsbury®

    1-inch plastic baby doll

1   can (12-ounce) whipped cream
    cheese frosting, *Pillsbury®*

    Green sanding sugar

    Purple sanding sugar

    Gold or yellow sanding sugar

1. Preheat oven to 400 degrees F. Line a baking sheet with parchment paper; set aside.

2. Unroll individual rolls. Loosely braid 3 rolls together; repeat with remaining rolls (there will be one roll left over). Pinch braids together to form one long braid. Loosely coil braid on the baking sheet, leaving a 3-inch hole in the center. Place the doll inside one of the braids. Bake in preheated oven for 16 to 20 minutes or until golden brown. Cool completely on wire rack.

3. In a small bowl, stir together icing from sweet rolls and the frosting. Frost cake; immediately sprinkle the sanding sugars on the frosting to form triangles of alternating colors.

Mardi Gras King Cakes are baked during Mardi Gras season, which is January 6 through Fat Tuesday. The cakes have a small plastic baby doll inside. King Cakes are served at gatherings where they're sliced and each person "searches for the baby." Custom holds that the person who finds the baby will be rewarded with good luck in the coming year (and is responsible for bringing the next cake to the next year's gathering). Cakes are decorated in the traditional Mardi Gras colors of purple (justice), green (faith), and gold (power).

Orange-Almond Tea Cakes

Prep 10 minutes   **Bake** 20 minutes   **Cool** 2 minutes   **Makes** 54 tea cakes

No-stick cooking spray, *Pam®*

FOR THE TEA CAKES:

1	**box (16-ounce) pound cake mix,** *Betty Crocker®*
1	**teaspoon pumpkin pie spice,** *McCormick®*
2	**large eggs**
¾	**cup orange juice,** *Minute Maid®*
½	**teaspoon orange extract,** *McCormick®*
¾	**cup slivered almonds, toasted and chopped,** *Planters®*

FOR GLAZE:

1	**cup powdered sugar,** *Domino®/C&H®*
1	**teaspoon orange zest**
3	**tablespoons orange juice,** *Minute Maid®*

1. Preheat oven to 350 degrees F. Spray mini muffin tins with baking spray; set aside.

2. For tea cakes, combine cake mix, pumpkin pie spice, eggs, orange juice, and orange extract; beat with an electric mixer on low speed for 30 seconds. Scrape bowl; beat on medium speed for 2 minutes. Stir in almonds. Spoon 1 tablespoon batter into each mini muffin cup (if necessary, bake in batches). Bake in preheated oven for 20 to 22 minutes or until a wooden toothpick inserted in the center comes out clean. Remove from muffin cups; cool on wire racks 2 to 4 minutes.

3. For glaze, in a small bowl, combine powdered sugar, orange zest, and orange juice; beat with an electric mixer for 30 seconds or until smooth. Dip tea cake tops into glaze mixture. Cool completely.

Fig and Raisin Crostata

Prep 15 minutes   **Bake** 20 minutes   **Cool** 10 minutes   **Makes** 8 servings

6   tablespoons lemon juice, *ReaLemon*®

1½   cup raisins, *Sun-Maid*®

1   tablespoon plus 1½ teaspoons sugar, *Domino*®/*C&H*®

¾   teaspoon salt

1   box (15-ounce) package of rolled refrigerated piecrust, *Pillsbury*®

4   ounces cream cheese, softened, *Philadelphia*®

4   fresh whole figs, sliced

     Honey

1   egg

1   teaspoon water

1. Preheat oven to 425 degrees F. Line a baking sheet with parchment paper; set aside.

2. In a food processor, combine lemon juice, raisins, sugar, and salt. Cover and process until mixture is a coarse paste; set aside.

3. On a lightly floured surface, sprinkle one piecrust with water. Place the second piecrust on top. Roll dough into a circle about 15 inches in diameter. Transfer piecrust to prepared baking sheet. Spread cream cheese over piecrust, leaving a 1-inch border; top with raisin mixture. Fold border up over filling; top with figs. Drizzle honey over figs.

4. In a small bowl, stir together egg and the water. Brush onto sides and the top of the piecrust. Bake in preheated oven for 20 to 25 minutes or until crust is golden and filling is bubbly. Cool on the baking sheet for 10 to 15 minutes.

Black Forest Napoleons

Prep 20 minutes   **Bake** 15 minutes   **Stand** 3 minutes   **Makes** 4 servings

1   sheet frozen puff pastry, thawed, *Pepperidge Farm*®

1   box (3.8-ounce) instant devil's food pudding and pie filling, *Jell-O*®

1½   cups milk

1   jar (10-ounce) maraschino cherries (reserve ½ cup juice), *Mariana*®

1   container (8-ounce) whipped dessert topping, thawed, *Cool Whip*®

2   tablespoons plus 1 teaspoon heavy cream

1½   cups powdered sugar, sifted, *Domino*®/*C&H*®

Chocolate syrup, *Hershey's*®

1. Preheat oven to 400 degrees F.

2. Unroll puff pastry sheet on lightly floured surface. Cut sheet into thirds along existing folds. Cut each third in half and then again in half for 12 total rectangles. Place 2 inches apart an ungreased baking sheet. Bake in preheated oven for 15 to 18 minutes or until golden. Remove from baking sheet; cool on wire rack.

3. In a large bowl, stir together pudding mix and milk for 2 minutes; let stand for 3 minutes to thicken. Refrigerate until ready to use.

4. Stir reserved cherry syrup into thawed whipped topping. Refrigerate until ready to use.

5. In a small bowl, stir heavy cream into powdered sugar until mixture is smooth. To assemble, split pastry rectangles in half horizontally. Place pastry bottoms on dessert plates. Spoon pudding mixture over pastry bottoms. Top each with another piece of pastry. Spread whipped topping over pastry. Top each with pastry top. Spread glaze over pastry. Drizzle each with chocolate syrup; top with a maraschino cherry.

Tapioca Corn Cobbler

Prep 10 minutes   **Cook** 3 hours (Low)   **Makes** 10 servings

No-stick cooking spray, *Pam®*

4   cups blue corn chips, *Garden of Eatin'®*

2   tablespoons butter, melted

1½   cups brown sugar, *Domino®/C&H®*

2   bags (16 ounces each) frozen mango chunks, thawed, *Dole®*

1   can (7-ounce) diced green chile peppers, *Ortega®*

2   to 3 red jalapeños, stemmed and seeded

2   tablespoons instant tapioca, *Minute®*

1. Spray a 4- to 5-quart slow cooker with cooking spray.

2. In a large bowl, crumble corn chips into small pieces. Add melted butter and ¼ cup brown sugar; stir.

3. In a large bowl, combine mango, chile peppers, jalapeños, tapioca, and remaining 1¼ cups brown sugar. Transfer to a 4- to 5-quart slow cooker. Sprinkle with corn chip mixture.

4. Cover and cook on Low heat setting for 3 to 4 hours.

Bahama Mama Cobbler

Prep 10 minutes   **Cook** 3 hours (Low)   **Makes** 10 servings

No-stick cooking spray, *Pam®*

1   bag (16-ounce) frozen mango chunks, thawed

1   can (20-ounce) pineapple chunks, drained, *Dole®*

2   large bananas, sliced 1 inch thick

2   tablespoons instant tapioca, *Minute®*

1½   teaspoons ground cinnamon, *McCormick®*

¼   cup dark rum, *Myers's®*

½   cup papaya nectar, *Kern's®*

2   tablespoons real maple syrup, *Spring Tree®*

1   package (12-ounce) coconut meringues, *Archway®*

1. Spray a 4- to 5-quart slow cooker with cooking spray.

2. In a large bowl, combine mango, pineapple, bananas, tapioca, and cinnamon. In a small bowl, stir together dark rum, nectar, and syrup; pour over fruit mixture. Stir to combine. Transfer to the slow cooker. Crumble meringues on top of fruit mixture.

3. Cover and cook on Low heat setting for 3 to 4 hours. Serve warm.

Amaretto Plums

Prep 10 minutes   Marinate 1 hour   Grill 6 minutes   Makes 6 servings

FOR THE PLUMS:

½   cup amaretto

2   tablespoons orange juice concentrate, *Minute Maid*®

6   whole cloves, *McCormick*®

6   ripe plums, quartered

FOR THE ALMOND MASCARPONE:

1   container (8-ounce) mascarpone, softened, *Cantare*®

½   cup slivered almonds, toasted, *Planters*®

1. For the plums, in a large zip-top bag, combine amaretto, orange juice concentrate, and cloves; reserve 2 tablespoons. Squeeze out air and seal. Gently massage bag to combine ingredients. Add plums; set aside. Marinate in the refrigerator for 1 to 4 hours.

2. For the almond mascarpone, in small bowl, combine the mascarpone, 2 tablespoons of reserved marinade, and ¼ cup almonds. Refrigerate until ready to use.

3. Set up grill for direct grilling over medium heat. Oil grate when ready to start cooking.

4. Remove plums from zip-top bag; discard marinade. Place plums on hot oiled grill. Grill for 3 to 4 minutes per side or until grill marks appear and plums begin to soften.

5. Serve warm plums with almond mascarpone. Garnish with remaining toasted almonds (optional).

Almond Rice Pudding

Prep 5 minutes   **Cook** 25 minutes   **Stand** 5 minutes   **Makes** 2 cups

1   cup instant rice, *Uncle Ben's*®
1   tablespoon butter
1   cup water
½   cup almond cake and pastry filling, *Solo*®
½   cup sugar, *Domino*®/*C&H*®
1½   cups milk
1   teaspoon cinnamon, *McCormick*®
1½   tablespoons lime juice, *Nellie & Joe's*®

1. In a medium saucepan, over medium-high heat, cook and stir rice, butter, and water. Bring to a rolling boil. Remove from heat. Cover and let sit for 5 minutes or until most of the water is absorbed. Stir in almond filling sugar, milk, and cinnamon; cover. Bring mixture to a boil, stirring occasionally. Uncover; simmer until mixture is creamy, about 20 minutes. Remove from heat; stir in lime juice. Serve warm or chilled.

Mudslide Pudding

Prep 10 minutes   **Stand** 9 minutes   **Makes** 6 servings

1   box (1.4-ounce) instant chocolate fudge pudding and pie filling, *Jell-O*®
3¾   cups milk
3   tablespoons coffee liqueur, *Kahlua*®
1   box (3.4-ounce) instant vanilla pudding and pie filling, *Jell-O*®
¼   cup Irish cream liqueur, *Baileys*®
1   box (1-ounce) instant white chocolate pudding and pie filling, *Jell-O*®
2   tablespoons vodka, *Smirnoff*®

1. In a medium bowl, whisk chocolate fudge pudding mix and 1¼ cups milk for 30 seconds. Add coffee liqueur. Whisk for 1½ minutes; let sit for 3 minutes. Cover with plastic wrap; refrigerate until ready to serve.

2. In a medium bowl, whisk vanilla pudding mix and 1¼ cups milk for 30 seconds. Add Irish cream liqueur. Whisk for 1½ minutes; let sit for 3 minutes. Cover with plastic wrap; refrigerate until ready to serve.

3. In a medium bowl, whisk white chocolate pudding mix and remaining 1¼ cups milk for 30 seconds. Add vodka. Whisk for 1½ minutes; let sit for 3 minutes. Cover with plastic wrap; refrigerate until ready to serve.

4. To serve, layer equal amounts of each pudding in six parfait glasses.

Orange Slice Cookies

Prep 45 minutes   **Bake** 10 minutes   **Makes** 18 cookies

¾   teaspoon orange extract, *McCormick®*

1   tablespoon orange zest

1   package (16.5-ounce) refrigerated sugar cookie dough, *Pillsbury®*

½   cup heavy cream

2   cups powdered sugar, sifted, *Domino®/C&H®*

4   drops yellow food coloring, *McCormick®*

2   drops red food coloring, *McCormick®*

½   cup orange decorating sugar

1   can (6.4-ounce) orange decorating icing, *Betty Crocker® Easy Flow*™

1. Preheat oven to 350 degrees F. Line 2 cookie sheets with parchment paper; set aside.

2. In a large bowl, knead ½ teaspoon orange extract and orange zest into dough. Roll dough into 18 balls. Place 2 inches apart on prepared cookie sheet. Dip the bottom of a drinking glass in *all-purpose flour*; flatten each ball to ¼ inch thickness. Bake in preheated oven for 10 to 12 minutes or until set on edges, rotating cookie sheets halfway through baking time. Transfer cookies to wire racks; let cool.

3. In a small bowl, stir cream into powdered sugar until a smooth glaze consistency. Stir in remaining orange extract and the yellow food coloring and the red food coloring. Pour decorating sugar into a small bowl. Dip outside edge of each cookie into glaze, then into decorating sugar. Place on wire cooling rack. Spread remaining glaze over the center of each cookie. Place on wire cooling rack to harden. Outline cookies with orange decorating icing; pipe segments on cookies.

Sunflower Brittle

Prep 10 minutes   **Bake** 10 minutes   **Cook** 25 minutes   **Cool** 30 minutes   **Yield** about 1 pound 6 ounces

1¾   cups shelled sunflower seeds, *Planters®*

1   tablespoon butter

1   cup brown sugar, *Domino®/C&H®*

1   cup dark corn syrup, *Karo®*

2   teaspoons baking soda

1. Preheat oven to 375 degrees F.

2. Spread sunflower seeds in a single layer on a baking sheet; bake for 10 to 12 minutes or until lightly browned. Cool on a wire rack.

3. Butter a 10×15-inch jelly-roll pan; set aside.

4. In a medium saucepan, combine brown sugar and corn syrup with a wooden spoon. Cook and stir over medium-high heat until mixture boils (about 8 minutes). Stir in sunflower seeds. Clip a candy thermometer to side of pan. Continue cooking, stirring occasionally, until thermometer registers 295 degrees F (about 12 minutes). Remove saucepan from heat; remove thermometer. Quickly stir in baking soda, stirring constantly. (The mixture will foam.) Immediately pour onto prepared baking sheet with the back of a spoon. Cool for 30 minutes. Invert baking sheet on a clean work surface; tap bottom of pan to loosen the brittle. Break into pieces.

Note: Store brittle in an air-tight container for up to 1 week.

Sassy Southern Style

Southern cooks are known for their good food, their ease in the kitchen, and their generous hospitality. No matter where you live, with these recipes for dishes such as Easy Chicken Gumbo and Beer Biscuits, Pan-Fried Catfish with Corn Tartar, and Sweet Potato Chops with Cajun Cream, you can be a Southern cook too.

Sweet Potato Chops
with Cajun Cream

Prep 10 minutes   Cook 4 minutes   Bake 30 minutes   Makes 4 servings

No-stick cooking spray, *Pam*®

1   bag microwave cut sweet potatoes, prepared according to package directions, *Ore-Ida*® *Steam 'n' Mash*™

1   tablespoon orange juice concentrate, *Minute Maid*®

1   teaspoon lemon juice, *Minute Maid*®

1   tablespoon butter

1   teaspoon salt

½   teaspoon minced ginger, *Gourmet Garden*®

⅓   cup crushed gingersnaps, *Nabisco*®

1   cup pecans, toasted and finely chopped, *Diamond*®

2   tablespoons melted butter

4   boneless, thin-cut pork loin chops

     Salt and ground black pepper

1   can (10-ounce) prepared white sauce, *Aunt Penny's*®

1   tablespoon bourbon, *Jim Beam*®

1½   teaspoons Cajun seasoning, *McCormick*®

1. Preheat oven to 350 degrees F. Spray a baking sheet with cooking spray; set aside.

2. In a large bowl, mash the prepared sweet potatoes with orange juice, lemon juice, butter, salt, and minced ginger; set aside to cool. In a small bowl, stir together the gingersnaps, pecans, and melted butter.

3. Rinse the pork chops and pat dry with paper towels. Place pork on prepared baking sheet and season with salt and pepper. Cover each chop with the sweet potato mixture and sprinkle with pecans. Bake in preheated oven for 30 to 40 minutes or until internal temperature reaches 150 degrees F.

4. Meanwhile, place white sauce in a medium microwave-safe bowl. Cover and microwave on high (100 percent power) for 2 minutes. Stir in bourbon and Cajun seasoning; cover and microwave for an additional 2 minutes. Serve chops with sauce.

Honeyed Peach Chops

Prep 10 minutes   **Marinate** 6 hours   **Cook** 35 minutes   **Bake** 27 minutes   **Makes** 6 servings   **Rest** 10 minutes

FOR THE TENDERLOINS:

8	**cups water**
1	**cup honey**
½	**cup kosher salt**
4	**tablespoons chopped garlic,** *Gourmet Garden*®
¼	**cup mixed pickling spice,** *McCormick*®
2	**pounds pork tenderloin, trimmed**
2	**tablespoons extra virgin olive oil**

FOR THE PEACHES:

1	**tablespoon extra virgin olive oil**
1	**bag (12-ounce) frozen pearl onions,** *Birds Eye*®
1	**cup cider vinegar**
2	**bags (10 ounces each) frozen sliced peaches,** *Cascadian Farm*®
3	**tablespoons Creole mustard,** *Zatarain's*®
½	**cup honey,** *Sue Bee*®
	Fresh sage leaves (optional)
	No-stick cooking spray, *Pam*®

1. For the tenderloins, in a medium saucepan, over high heat, combine 2 cups of the water, honey, salt, 3 tablespoons garlic, and pickling spice. Bring to a boil; remove from heat, add the remaining 6 cups of water, and cool to room temperature. Place the pork in a large plastic container and pour in the cooled brine, making sure that it completely covers the pork. Cover with a tight-fitting lid and refrigerate for 6 to 8 hours, no longer.

2. For the peaches, in a large saucepan, over medium-high heat, heat the oil. Add the onions and remaining 1 tablespoon garlic, stirring constantly. Reduce the heat to medium heat and cook and stir for 10 minutes or until the onions are translucent. Increase heat to medium-high; add the vinegar, peaches, mustard, and honey. Simmer for 20 minutes or until the sauce has thickened, stirring occasionally. Remove from heat; set aside to cool.

3. Preheat oven to 475 degrees F. Line a roasting pan with foil and spray the foil with cooking spray. Remove the pork from the brine; discard the brine. Dry the pork with paper towels. Rub the pork with oil and place in the prepared roasting pan. Bake for 12 minutes, turning once to brown both sides. Bake for 15 to 20 minutes more or until internal temperature reaches 150 degrees F. Remove from oven and let pork rest for about 10 minutes. Slice the pork and serve with the peaches. Garnish with fresh sage leaves (optional).

NOTE: Store extra Creole Mustard Peaches in the refrigerator, covered, for up to 1 month. Serve with bratwurst or roasted or fried chicken.

Aïoli Pork Sliders

Prep 20 minutes   **Cook** 4 minutes   **Makes** 4 servings

FOR THE SPICY AÏOLI:

1¼   cups mayonnaise, *Best Foods®*

1   teaspoon Cajun seasoning, *McCormick®*

1   scallion, finely chopped

½   teaspoon crushed garlic, *Gourmet Garden®*

2½   teaspoons lemon juice, *ReaLemon®*

FOR THE SLIDERS:

1¼   pounds pork tenderloin, trimmed, sliced 1 inch thick

1   box (8.5-ounce) corn muffin mix, *Jiffy®*

2   tablespoons Cajun seasoning, *McCormick®*

1   egg

½   cup all-purpose flour

  Canola oil

  White dinner rolls or buns

  Butterhead lettuce

  Sliced tomatoes

  Sliced red onions

1. For the spicy aïoli, in a small bowl, stir together mayonnaise, Cajun seasoning, scallion, garlic, and lemon juice; cover and refrigerate until ready to serve.

2. For the sliders, place pork between two pieces of plastic wrap. Using the flat side of a meat mallet, pound pork until ¼ inch to ⅛ inch thick. Remove plastic wrap; set aside. In a medium bowl, combine muffin mix and Cajun seasoning; set aside. In a small bowl, lightly beat egg with 1 tablespoon *water;* set aside. Place the flour in a shallow dish or pie plate. Coat both sides of the pork in the flour; then dip into the egg wash and coat in the muffin mixture. Place pork on a plate.

3. In a large skillet, over medium to medium-high heat, heat ¼ inch of oil. Oil is ready for frying when a drop of water splatters when dropped in. Without crowding pan, fry pork until golden brown, about 2 to 3 minutes on each side. Serve pork on split buns spread with aïoli; top with lettuce, tomatoes, and onions.

Zesty Jambalaya

Prep 10 minutes   Cook 25 minutes   Stand 5 minutes   Makes 4 servings

1   tablespoon extra virgin olive oil

1   cup diced frozen onion, thawed
     and drained, *Ore-Ida*®

1   tablespoon crushed garlic,
     Gourmet Garden®

1   pound boneless pork loin, cut into
     ¼-inch cubes

8   ounces Andouille sausage, cut into
     ¼-inch slices

2   cups low-sodium chicken broth,
     Swanson®

1   can (10-ounce) diced tomatoes
     and green chiles, *Ro Tel*®

1   package (8-ounce) jambalaya mix,
     Zatarain's®

1   jar (6.5-ounce) diced pimientos,
     drained, *Dromedary*®

1   pinch ground cloves, *McCormick*®

1. In a Dutch oven, over medium-high heat, heat the oil. Add the onion and garlic and cook and stir for 5 minutes or until the onion is softened. Add the pork and sausage and cook and stir for another 5 minutes or until the meat is browned. Add the broth and bring to a boil. Stir in diced tomatoes, jambalaya mix, pimientos, and cloves and return to a boil. Reduce heat and simmer, covered, for 15 minutes. Let stand 5 minutes before serving.

Creole Chicken

Prep 10 minutes   **Stand** 10 minutes   **Cook** 3 minutes   **Makes** 4 servings

4   tablespoons all-purpose flour

1   tablespoon ground black pepper

2   teaspoons Creole seasoning, *ony Chachere's*®

1   teaspoon dried thyme, *McCormick*®

4   boneless, skinless chicken cutlets

1½   tablespoons extra virgin olive oil

1½   tablespoons unsalted butter

1   bottle (7.20-ounce) bold and spicy Creole sauce, *Crosse and Blackwell*®

Dirty rice, prepared according to package directions, *Zatarain's*® (optional)

Steamed okra (optional)

1. In a shallow dish, combine flour, pepper, Creole seasoning, and thyme. Coat each cutlet in flour mixture, tapping off any excess. Place cutlets on a plate and let stand for 10 minutes.

2. In a large skillet, over medium-high heat, heat oil and butter. Add chicken to skillet and cook for 5 to 7 minutes or until cutlets are crisp and no longer pink inside, turning once. Top each cutlet with 3 tablespoons of Creole sauce. Serve with dirty rice and steamed okra (optional).

Easy Chicken Gumbo
and Beer Biscuits

Prep 15 minutes   **Cook** 30 minutes   **Bake** 8 minutes   **Makes** 8 servings

FOR THE GUMBO:

2   tablespoons canola oil

1½   cups frozen chopped onions,
       thawed, *Ore-Ida*®

2   stalks celery, diced

½   cup frozen chopped green peppers,
       Pictsweet®

1   package (16-ounce) frozen cut
       okra, *Pictsweet*®

3   cans (14 ounces each) low-sodium
       chicken broth, *Swanson*®

1   box (4.5-ounce) gumbo base,
       Zatarain's®

1   rotisserie chicken, chopped

1   can (15-ounce) red kidney beans,
       drained, *S&W*®

2   tablespoons seafood seasoning,
       Old Bay®

FOR THE BISCUITS:

⅔   bottle (12-ounce) beer

2¼   cups biscuit mix, plus extra for
       dusting, *Pioneer*®

1   teaspoon ground black pepper

2   tablespoons sugar, *Domino*®/*C&H*®

1. Preheat oven to 375 degrees F.

2. For the gumbo, in a stockpot, over medium-high heat, heat oil. Add onions, celery, chopped peppers, and okra and cook for 3 to 4 minutes. Add broth and gumbo base and bring to a boil. Add chicken, beans, and seafood seasoning. Simmer, covered, for 30 minutes.

3. For the biscuits, in a large mixing bowl, combine beer, biscuit mix, pepper, and sugar. Drop by spoonfuls into 10 mounds onto baking sheet. Bake for 8 to 10 minutes or until golden brown.

Cajun Turkey Burgers

Prep 15 minutes   **Cook** 10 minutes   **Makes** 4 servings

2   tablespoons thinly sliced scallions

3   tablespoons celery, coarsely chopped

¼   cup roasted red peppers, *Delallo®*

2   tablespoons chopped fresh parsley

1   tablespoon **Cajun seasoning**, *McCormick®*

1¼   pounds ground turkey

3   tablespoons plus ¼ cup tartar sauce, *Hellmann's®*

¼   cup plain bread crumbs, *Progresso®*

1   large egg, beaten

       Kosher salt and ground black pepper

       Hot sauce, *Tabasco* sauce® (optional)

1   roma tomato, diced

1   teaspoon garlic blend, *Gourmet Garden®*

4   hamburger buns, toasted

       Leaf lettuce

       Red onion, sliced

1. In a food processor, combine the scallions, celery, red peppers, parsley, and Cajun seasoning. Cover and process until smooth. Transfer mixture to a large bowl. Add turkey, 3 tablespoons tartar sauce, bread crumbs, and egg; mix well. Season with salt, pepper, and hot sauce (optional). Shape turkey mixture into four 4-inch patties.

2. Preheat broiler. Place patties on a foil-lined baking sheet or broiler pan. Broil 6 to 8 inches from the heat for 5 to 7 minutes on each side until internal temperature reaches 165 degrees F.

3. In a small bowl, stir together remaining ¼ cup tartar sauce, diced tomato, and garlic. Serve patties on toasted hamburger buns with lettuce, red onion, and tartar sauce mixture.

Pan-Fried Catfish
with Corn Tartar

Prep 15 minutes   **Cook** 4 minutes   **Makes** 4 servings

FOR THE TARTAR SAUCE:

½ cup hot chowchow, drained, *Mrs. Renfro's*®

1 cup frozen niblets corn, thawed, *Green Giant*®

½ cup mayonnaise

FOR THE CATFISH:

1½ pounds fresh catfish fillets

1 box (6-ounce) cornmeal stuffing mix, *Stove Top*®

½ cup all-purpose flour

1 teaspoon salt

1 teaspoon ground black pepper

2 large eggs

2 tablespoons water

3 cups vegetable oil

1. For the tartar sauce, in a serving bowl, combine the chowchow, corn, and mayonnaise; set aside.

2. For the catfish, rinse catfish under cold water and pat dry with paper towels. In a food processor, process the stuffing mix until finely ground; pour into a shallow dish or pie plate. In large zip-top bag, combine the flour, salt, and pepper. Add the fish and turn to coat the fish. Shake off any excess flour and place on a baking sheet lined with paper towels.

3. Beat eggs and water in a shallow dish or pie plate. Dip the catfish in the egg mixture; then coat in the stuffing mix. Shake off any excess crumbs and place on the prepared baking sheet. In a large skillet, over medium-high heat, heat the oil to 350 degrees F. Add the catfish and cook for about 2 minutes on each side or until the fish is golden brown and begins to flake when tested with a fork. Remove fish and drain on paper towels. Serve with the tartar sauce.

Bayou Bounty Alfredo

Prep 5 minutes   **Cook** 10 minutes   **Makes** 4 servings

3	tablespoons unsalted butter
2	tablespoons minced garlic, *Gourmet Garden*®
½	pound cooked, peeled shrimp, any size
1	pound cooked crawfish, thawed
1	packet (1.6-ounce) Alfredo sauce mix, *Knorr*®
1	teaspoon seafood seasoning, *Old Bay*®
2	cups milk
½	cup grated Parmesan cheese
3	tablespoons chopped fresh parsley
	Kosher salt
1	pound fettuccine pasta, cooked according to package directions, *DeCecco*®

1. In a large skillet, over medium-high heat, heat the butter. Cook and stir garlic for 2 minutes. Add the shrimp and crawfish and cook another 4 minutes or until the seafood is heated through. Stir in the sauce mix, seasoning, and milk. Cook for 2 more minutes or until thickened, stirring constantly. Sprinkle with Parmesan cheese, about 1 tablespoon at a time. Add the parsley and salt. Toss with pasta.

Hushpuppy Poppers

Prep 20 minutes   **Stand** 15 minutes   **Bake** 10 minutes   **Makes** 18 cookies

	No-stick cooking spray, *Pam*®
2	tablespoons bacon fat or vegetable shortening
¼	cup butter, softened
2	cups yellow cornmeal, *Albers*®
1	medium yellow onion, diced
1	cup baking mix, *Bisquick*®
1½	teaspoons baking powder
1	teaspoon seafood seasoning, *Old Bay*®
¼	teaspoon ground black pepper
2	tablespoons granulated sugar, *Domino*®/*C&H*®
¼	cup buttermilk
2	tablespoons water
1	egg, beaten
¼	cup finely chopped fresh parsley
¼	cup real bacon pieces, *Hormel*®

1. Preheat oven to 350 degrees F. Lightly spray two baking sheets with cooking spray; set aside.

2. In a medium mixing bowl, beat the bacon fat and butter until light. Add the cornmeal and beat with an electric mixer on low speed until thoroughly combined; mixture will be crumbly. Add the onion and baking mix, beating on low speed after each addition. Stir in the baking powder, seafood seasoning, pepper, sugar, buttermilk, water, egg, parsley, and bacon pieces. Let the batter rest for 15 minutes.

3. Using a small scoop, drop the batter 2 inches apart on the prepared baking sheets. Bake for 10 to 15 minutes or until golden brown. Serve hot.

Arugula Peach Salad

Start to Finish 15 minutes   **Makes** 4 servings

1	teaspoon minced garlic, *Gourmet Garden*®
3	cups mixed salad greens, *Fresh Express*®
1	cup arugula, *Fresh Express*®
3	tablespoons extra virgin olive oil
½	teaspoon kosher salt
2	cups frozen peaches, thawed, *Dole*®
½	small red onion, thinly sliced, rinsed in cold water, and drained
¼	cup pitted kalamata olives, *Peloponnese*®
12	large basil leaves
	Newman's Own® *Balsamic Natural Salad Mist*

1. Rub the garlic inside a wooden salad bowl. Add the mixed greens and arugula and toss with the oil and salt; set aside. Add the peaches, onion, and olives. To chiffonade the basil, stack the basil leaves on top of each other and roll them up lengthwise. Thinly slice the leaves. Add the basil to the greens and toss. Divide salad among serving 4 plates and spray with salad mist.

American Classics

There are certain dishes that everyone—no matter where they live and what they grew up eating—holds as favorite foods. They're the hearty, soul-warming dishes of potlucks and church suppers: meat loaf, shepherd's pie, oven-fried chicken. It's the kind of food that brings the whole gang to the table and leaves them feeling happy and content.

Red Eye Texas T-Bone

Prep 10 minutes   Marinate 1 hour   Cook 20 minutes   Stand 10 minutes   Makes 4 servings

FOR THE T-BONES:

4   T-bone steaks (10 to 12 ounces each)

1½   teaspoons kosher salt

1   teaspoon coarsely ground black pepper

2   tablespoons finely ground coffee

¼   cup firmly packed brown sugar, *Domino®/C&H®*

1   tablespoon chopped garlic, *Gourmet Garden®*

2   teaspoons mesquite seasoning mix, *McCormick® Grill Mates®*

1   tablespoon chipotle cinnamon rub, *McCormick® Gourmet Collection*

¼   cup olive oil

FOR THE GRAVY:

1   cup brewed strong black coffee

1   cup beef consommé, *Campbells®*

½   cup coffee-flavored liqueur, *Kahlua®*

¼   cup jalapeño jelly, *Tabasco®*

1   tablespoon chopped garlic, *Gourmet Garden®*

1   teaspoon coarsely ground black pepper

2   teaspoons heavy cream

1. Preheat oven to 450 degrees F.

2. For the T-bones, rinse and pat steaks dry with paper towels. Rub with salt and pepper. In a small bowl, combine the ground coffee, sugar, garlic, mesquite seasoning, and chipotle cinnamon rub. Rub coffee mixture into the steaks. Place steaks in a large zip-top plastic bag. Squeeze out air and seal. Marinate in the refrigerator for 1 hour.

3. Heat two large ovenproof skillets over high heat. Add 2 tablespoons oil to each skillet; when the oil begins to smoke, add the steaks. Reduce heat to medium-high heat and brown the steaks for 4 minutes on each side. Transfer skillets to the oven. Roast for 6 to 8 minutes (135 degrees F for medium-rare). Transfer steaks to a platter, reserving drippings in the skillet, and let stand for 10 minutes.

4. For the gravy, heat one of the skillets over high heat; add the coffee and consommé; stir to scrape up the brown bits. Remove from heat. Heat the other skillet over high heat; add the coffee mixture from the first skillet and stir to scrape up the brown bits. Whisk in the coffee liqueur, jelly, garlic, and pepper. Reduce the sauce by half, about 10 minutes. Remove from the heat and stir in the cream. To serve, pour sauce on serving plate and top with the steaks.

Honey Mustard Pretzel Tenderloin

Prep 15 minutes　　**Stand** 20 minutes　　**Bake** 20 minutes　　**Makes** 4 servings

1	tablespoon olive oil
1	2-pound center portion beef tenderloin, trimmed
2	teaspoons ground black pepper
1	tablespoon chopped garlic, *Gourmet Garden*®
¼	cup coarse-grain mustard, *Ingelhoffer*®
¼	cup Dijon mustard, *Ingelhoffer*®
¼	cup honey, *Sue Bee*®
2	tablespoons brown sugar, *Domino*®/*C&H*®
2	cups crushed salted pretzels
4	tablespoons unsalted butter
	Mustards

1. Preheat oven to 500 degrees F. In a large nonstick skillet, heat oil over high heat. Rub meat with black pepper and brown quickly on all sides. Remove from skillet; set aside.

2. In a small bowl, combine the garlic, coarse-grain mustard, Dijon mustard, honey, and brown sugar. Rub the mustard mixture all over the roast. Place the crushed pretzels in a large shallow dish. Roll the roast in the pretzels, pressing firmly. Let stand for 10 to 15 minutes. Heat a large nonstick roasting pan in the oven; add butter. When the butter has melted, place the roast in the pan, turning quickly to coat all sides with butter. Return pan to the oven and reduce oven temperature to 375 degrees F. Bake, turning occasionally, for 20 to 25 minutes (135 degrees F for medium-rare). Remove roast from oven and loosely cover with foil. Let stand for 10 to 15 minutes. Serve sliced with a selection of mustards.

Competition Chili

Prep 15 minutes   Cook 2 hours   Makes 6 servings

3   tablespoons olive oil

2   pounds trimmed beef stew meat,
        cut into ½-inch pieces

3   teaspoons kosher salt

1   large yellow onion, chopped

3   tablespoons minced garlic,
        Gourmet Garden®

2   tablespoons chopped pickled
        jalapeño chiles, *Ortega*®

1   packet (1.25-ounce) chili seasoning
        mix, *McCormick*®

2   tablespoons smoky sweet pepper
        seasoning blend, *McCormick*®

1   tablespoon coarsely ground black
        pepper

¼   cup mole paste, *Doña Maria*®

1   bottle (12-ounce) dark beer,
        Shiner® *Bock* or *Sam Adams*® *Lager*

2½   cups beef broth, *Swanson*®

        Grated cheddar cheese

        Chopped yellow onion

        Hot sauce, *Tabasco*®

        Saltine crackers, *Nabisco*®

1. In a 12-quart stockpot, over high heat, heat the olive oil. Add the meat and season with 2 teaspoons of the salt; cook and stir for 6 to 7 minutes or until the meat has just turned brown. Add onion and 1 tablespoon of the garlic and cook for another 5 minutes or until onions are limp. Stir in the jalapeño, chili seasoning, pepper blend, remaining 2 tablespoons garlic, remaining 1 teaspoon salt, and black pepper. Stir in the mole paste, beer, and broth and bring to a boil. Reduce heat to medium-low heat and cook, covered, for 2 to 4 hours, stirring occasionally. Serve in large soup bowls with cheese, onion, hot sauce, and crackers.

Beefy Stroganoff

Prep 10 minutes   Cook 20 minutes   Makes 4 servings

2   tablespoons extra virgin olive oil

1   yellow onion, thinly sliced

1   teaspoon granulated sugar, *Domino®/C&H®*

1   package (8-ounce) sliced mushrooms

1   tablespoon minced garlic, *Gourmet Garden®*

4   cups wide egg noodles

3   bags (3 ounces each) refrigerated seasoned beef strips, *Tyson®*

1   package (1.2-ounce) brown gravy mix, *Knorr®*

½   teaspoon ground black pepper

1   cup cold water

1   cup low-fat sour cream

1. In a large skillet, heat the oil over medium-high heat. Add the onion and sugar; reduce the heat to medium and cook for 10 minutes or until onion starts to caramelize. Add mushrooms and garlic and cook for another 5 minutes or until tender.

2. Meanwhile, cook noodles according to package directions. Add the beef to the mushrooms and onion and cook for 3 to 5 minutes or until heated through. In a small bowl, combine the gravy mix, pepper, and water; mix well. Stir sauce mixture into beef and mushrooms, stirring constantly, until sauce comes to a boil. Reduce heat to a simmer, stirring frequently. Cook for 1 minute or until thickened. Remove from heat and stir in ½ cup of the sour cream. Serve stroganoff over warm noodles. Top with remaining sour cream (optional).

Bacon-Blessed Meat Loaf

Prep 20 minutes   **Bake** 50 minutes   **Makes** 6 servings

No-stick cooking spray, *Pam*®

24   whole roasted garlic cloves, *Gourmet Garden*®

1   pound ground beef

1   pound ground turkey or veal

1   pound ground pork

½   cup grated yellow onion

1   packet (1.12-ounce) meat loaf seasoning mix, *McCormick*®

½   cup tomato ketchup, *Heinz*®

1   cup fresh plain bread crumbs

1   egg

1   teaspoon ground black pepper

¼   cup finely chopped fresh flat-leaf parsley

¼   cup Dijon mustard, *Ingelhoffer*®

3   tablespoons brown sugar

8   slices thinly sliced bacon

1. Heat oven to 350 degrees F. Line a rimmed baking sheet with foil and spray with cooking spray; set aside.

2. In a large mixing bowl, combine the garlic cloves, beef, turkey, pork, onion, meat loaf seasoning mix, ketchup, bread crumbs, egg, black pepper, and parsley. Mix with a rubber spatula or clean hands just until the ingredients are combined. Turn the meat mixture out onto the prepared baking sheet and shape into a large loaf. Or divide the mixture into 4 to 6 equal portions and shape into individual meat loaves. Spread the mustard over the top of the meat loaf and sprinkle with brown sugar. Wrap bacon around the meat loaf, tucking in the ends. Bake the meat loaf for 50 to 60 minutes for one large loaf or 25 to 35 minutes for the smaller loaves or until internal temperature reaches 160 degrees F.

Beer Brat Bake

Prep 10 minutes   Cook 5 minutes   Bake 1 hour 15 minutes   Makes 6 servings

No-stick cooking spray, *Pam®*

1   package (16-ounce) cooked bratwurst, *Johnsonville®*

1   cup frozen seasoning blend, *Pictsweet®*

1   can (10-ounce) diced tomatoes and green chiles, *Ro-Tel®*

2   cups diced cooked potatoes, *Reser's®*

1   box (6.3-ounce) country cheddar rice mix, *Rice-A-Roni®*

1   bottle (12-ounce) beer

1   cup chicken broth, *Swanson®*

1   tablespoon crushed garlic, *Gourmet Garden®*

½   teaspoon dried marjoram, *McCormick®*

Shredded Parmesan cheese, *DiGiorno®*

1. Preheat oven to 350 degrees F. Spray a 2½-quart casserole dish with cooking spray; set aside.

2. In a large skillet, over medium heat, brown the bratwurst. Remove from the skillet and cool for 15 minutes. Slice into 1-inch pieces. In the prepared casserole dish, combine the bratwurst, seasoning blend, diced tomatoes, potatoes, and rice mix. In a medium bowl, stir together the rice seasoning packet, beer, chicken broth, garlic, and marjoram. Pour into the casserole dish and stir until well combined. Cover dish with a lid or foil. Bake in the preheated oven for 75 to 90 minutes or until rice is cooked. Sprinkle individual servings with the Parmesan cheese.

Crispy Oven Potato-Flaked Chicken

Prep 15 minutes   **Stand** 20 minutes   **Bake** 30 minutes   **Makes** 4 servings

No-stick cooking spray, *Pam®*

2   whole eggs, beaten

½   cup chicken broth, *Swanson®*

Ground black pepper

2   packages (3.5 ounces each) instant roasted garlic mashed potato flakes, *Hungry Jack®*

1   whole chicken, cut up, skin removed

1. Preheat oven to 425 degrees F. Spray a baking sheet with cooking spray; set aside.

2. In a medium bowl, combine the eggs, broth, and black pepper. Place the potato flakes in a shallow dish. Dip the chicken in the egg mixture, then coat with the potato flakes. Place on the prepared baking sheet about 1 inch apart. Let stand for 20 minutes. Spray with cooking spray. Bake for 30 to 45 minutes or until golden brown.

Chicken Shepherd's Pie

Prep 10 minutes   **Cook** 10 minutes   **Bake** 30 minutes   **Makes** 8 servings

No-stick cooking spray, *Pam®*

2 pounds boneless, skinless chicken breasts, cut into bite-size pieces

2 teaspoons salt-free chicken seasoning, *McCormick® Grill Mates®*

2 tablespoons canola oil

1 medium yellow onion, finely chopped

2 teaspoons garlic blend, *Gourmet Garden®*

1 bag (16-ounce) frozen mixed vegetables (carrots, corn, peas, green beans), thawed, *C&W®*

2 cans (10 ounces each) condensed cream of chicken soup, *Campbell's®*

1 bag (24-ounce) frozen cut russet potatoes, *Ore-Ida® Steam & Mash*

⅔ cup milk

2 tablespoons butter

¼ cup seasoned bread crumbs, *Progresso®*

1. Preheat oven to 350 degrees F. Lightly spray a shallow 9×13-inch baking dish with cooking spray; set aside. Season chicken with chicken seasoning; set aside.

2. In a large skillet, over medium-high heat, heat oil. Add chicken and cook for 3 to 4 minutes or until chicken is no longer pink. Add onions and garlic and cook and stir for 2 minutes. Stir in vegetables and soup; cook until heated through. Transfer to the prepared baking dish.

3. Microwave potatoes according to package directions. In a medium bowl, mash potatoes with milk and butter. Spread potato mixture evenly over chicken and vegetable mixture. Sprinkle bread crumbs. Bake in preheated oven for 30 to 45 minutes or until hot and bubbly.

Mom's Macaroni Salad

Prep 10 minutes   **Chill** 1 hour   **Makes** 6 servings

2   cups mayonnaise, *Best Foods*®

3   tablespoons Dijon mustard, *Grey Poupon*®

1   packet (2.15-ounce) vegetable soup mix, *Knorr*®

2   tablespoons granulated sugar, *Domino*®/*C&H*®

1   tablespoon cider vinegar, *Heinz*®

1½   teaspoons celery seeds

1   teaspoon salt

2   cups shredded carrots, *Ready Pac*®

3   hard-cooked eggs, from the deli, chopped

1   small yellow onion, diced

1   jar (4-ounce) chopped red pimientos, drained, *Dromedary*®

2   tablespoons sweet pickle juice

2   cups uncooked elbow macaroni, cooked according to package directions, *Barilla*®

Celery leaves for garnish (optional)

1. In a large bowl, stir together mayonnaise, mustard, soup mix, sugar, vinegar, celery seeds, and salt. Stir in the carrots, eggs, onion, pimientos, and pickle juice. Stir in cooked macaroni. Cover and chill for at least 1 hour. Garnish with celerly leaves (optional).

Broccoli Cheese Casserole

Prep 5 minutes   **Bake** 40 minutes   **Makes** 5 servings

No-stick cooking spray, *Pam*®

1   can (10.75-ounce) condensed cheddar cheese soup, *Campbell's*®

½   cup milk

2   tablespoons butter, melted

1   box (6.2-ounce) long grain and wild rice, *Uncle Ben's*®

1   cup seasoning blend, *PictSweet*®

1   bag (14-ounce) frozen broccoli florets, thawed, *C&W*®

½   cup shredded cheddar-jack cheese, *Sargento*®

1. Preheat oven to 350 degrees F. Spray a 1½-quart casserole dish with cooking spray; set aside.

2. In a large bowl, stir together cheddar cheese soup, milk, and butter until combined. Stir in rice, seasoning blend, and broccoli. Pour into prepared casserole dish. Top with shredded cheese. Bake in preheated oven for 40 to 45 minutes.

Scalloped Chive Potatoes

Prep 10 minutes   **Cook** 7 minutes   **Bake** 35 minutes   **Makes** 6 servings

4   tablespoons butter

½   cup frozen chopped onion, *Ore-Ida*®

¼   cup fresh chives, chopped

1   package (16-ounce) frozen O'Brien potatoes, *Ore-Ida*®

½   cup bottled roasted red peppers, chopped, *Delallo*®

1   can (10.5-ounce) condensed cream of celery soup, *Campbell's*®

½   cup shredded cheddar cheese, *Sargento*®

½   cup shredded provolone cheese, *Sargento*®

½   cup milk

½   teaspoon ground black pepper

1   cup crushed crackers, *Ritz*®

1. Preheat oven to 375 degrees F. In a large ovenproof skillet, over medium-high heat, melt butter. Cook and stir onions until translucent. Stir in chives, potatoes, red peppers, soup, cheddar cheese, provolone cheese, milk, black pepper, and ½ cup of the cracker crumbs.

2. Place the skillet in the oven (or transfer potatoes to a buttered 2-quart casserole) and top with remaining ½ cup cracker crumbs. Bake in the preheated oven for 35 to 40 minutes or until golden brown.

Note: Assemble this dish the day before and refrigerate until ready to bake. Before baking, let the pan sit out for 30 minutes to warm up, top with cracker crumbs, and bake 50 to 60 minutes or until golden brown.

Family Snacks and Finger Foods

Whether you're throwing a party or simply settling in with the family for movie night, offering something yummy to nibble on adds to the fun. Having the recipes for these quick, easy snacks at your fingertips means you can make and serve something really delicious in not much more time than it takes to open a bag of chips!

Oven-Fried Party Drummettes

Prep 10 minutes   **Bake** 40 minutes   **Makes** 16 servings

3   pounds chicken drummettes

2   teaspoons garlic-pepper blend, *McCormick®*

1   packet (1.0-ounce) ranch dressing mix, *Hidden Valley®*

¾   cup all-purpose flour

½   cup butter

1   cup buttermilk ranch salad dressing, *Hidden Valley®*

1   teaspoon hot pepper sauce, plus more to taste, *Tabasco®*

1. Preheat oven to 425 degrees F.

2. Sprinkle all sides of drummettes with garlic pepper; set aside.

3. In a large zip-top bag, combine the dressing mix and the flour; mix well. Add drummettes and shake until coated. Place the butter on a rimmed baking sheet. Place in oven until butter melts and begins to sizzle. Add drummettes to pan and bake for 20 minutes. Turn drummettes and bake for another 20 minutes or until golden brown.

4. Stir together the salad dressing and hot pepper sauce. Refrigerate until ready to serve.

Shrimp Toasties

Prep 15 minutes   **Cook** 4 minutes   **Bake** 15 minutes   **Makes** 32 toasties

1   bag (16-ounce) Hawaiian sweet bread, *King's®*
       Butter-flavored cooking spray, *Pam®*

1   tablespoon sesame oil, *Dynasty®*

1   teaspoon crushed garlic, *Garden Gourmet®*

2   cups frozen, peeled, and deveined, medium (41 to 50 count) shrimp (no tails), thawed and chopped, *Contessa®*

2   teaspoons soy sauce, *Kikkoman®*

1   tablespoon lemon juice, *Minute Maid®*

2   teaspoons rice vinegar, *Marukan®*

¼   cup mayonnaise, *Best Foods®* or *Hellmann's®*

2   tablespoons cilantro, finely chopped

1. Preheat oven to 350 degrees F. Trim top and sides of bread to make a rectangular loaf. Cut 8 slices from the loaf; cut each slice in half. Cut each half diagonally to make four triangles. Repeat to make 32 triangles. Place bread on 2 baking sheets; spray bread with cooking spray. Bake in the preheated oven for 10 minutes or until golden. Cool on a wire rack. Increase oven temperature to 375 degrees F. In a large saucepan, over medium-high heat, heat the oil. Add the garlic and shrimp and cook and stir for 2 minutes. Stir in soy sauce, lemon juice, and rice vinegar and cook for 2 minutes. Remove from heat and spoon into a bowl. Stir in mayonnaise and cilantro. Spoon shrimp mixture onto the bread. Bake for 5 minutes or until mixture is heated through and bread is golden brown.

Chicken Jerkabobs

Prep 15 minutes **Marinate** 1 hour **Grill** 10 minutes **Makes** 12 servings

2	pounds chicken breasts, cut into 1½ inch pieces
¼	cup orange juice, *Minute Maid®*
¼	cup honey, *Sue Bee®*
1	tablespoon olive oil
2	tablespoons Jamaican jerk seasoning, *The Spice Hunter®*
1	tablespoon dark rum, *Meyers's®* (optional)
1	red bell pepper, cut into 2-inch chunks
1	yellow bell pepper, cut into 2-inch chunks
1	package (8-ounce) mushrooms, trimmed
2	small red onions, cut into sixths, leaving root end intact

1. Place chicken in a large zip-lock bag; add the orange juice, honey, oil, jerk seasoning, and rum. Squeeze out air and seal. Gently massage bag to combine ingredients. Marinate in the refrigerator for 1 to 3 hours.

2. Soak 10-inch wooden skewers in water for at least 1 hour. Set up the grill for direct cooking over high heat. *Oil* grate when ready to start cooking. Remove chicken from the marinade; discard marinade. Thread chicken, peppers, mushrooms, and onions onto skewers. Place skewers on hot oiled grill. Cook for 5 to 8 minutes per side or until chicken is no longer pink and internal temperature reaches 160 degrees F.

Salmon Sushi Bites

Prep 15 minutes **Cook** 5 minutes **Makes** 24 bites

1½	cups instant rice, *Uncle Ben's®*
1½	cups water
1½	teaspoons rice vinegar, *Marukan®*
1	tablespoon sugar, *Domino®/C&H®*
¾	teaspoon salt-free all-purpose seasoning, *McCormick®*
	Pinch salt
3	packages (4 ounces each) sliced smoked salmon, *Three Star®*
	Sesame seeds (optional)
	Soy sauce, *Kikkoman®*

1. In a small saucepan, over high heat, bring rice and water to a boil. Reduce heat; cover and simmer for 5 minutes or until all water is absorbed. Stir in vinegar, sugar, seasoning, and salt.

2. On a cutting board, separate slices of salmon and cut into 1½-inch strips. Place 2 teaspoons of rice at one end of each salmon strip. Roll up tightly. Sprinkle with sesame seeds (optional). Serve sushi bites with soy sauce for dipping.

Crispy Potato Poppers

Prep 10 minutes   Cook 10 minutes   Makes 30 poppers

Oil

1   container (21-ounce) loaded mashed potatoes, *Country Crock®*

1   tablespoon butter

1   egg

½   cup shredded Romano cheese, *DiGiorno®*

1   cup all-purpose flour

1. In a medium saucepan, heat 1 inch of oil to 350 degrees F.

2. Place potatoes and butter in a microwave-safe bowl. Cover and microwave on high setting (100 percent power) for 2½ minutes. Transfer potato mixture to a large bowl; add egg, cheese, and flour. Stir to combine. Shape into 1-inch balls. Working in batches, fry potato balls 3 minutes per side or until golden brown. Remove with a slotted spoon and drain on paper towels.

Orange Soda Ceviche

Prep 15 minutes   Cook 4 minutes   Chill 3 hours   Makes 4 servings

1   pound skinless red snapper fillets

1   pound precooked medium (41 to 50 count) shrimp, peeled and deveined (no tails), *Contessa®*

1   package (0.07-ounce) Italian dressing mix, *Good Seasons®*

1   cup lime juice, *ReaLime®*

1   cup orange soda, *Sunkist®*

1   medium yellow onion, diced

1   whole avocado, pitted, peeled, and chopped

1   tablespoon chopped garlic, *Gourmet Garden®*

1   tablespoon diced jalapeño, *Ortega®*

½   cup chopped fresh cilantro

1   cup tomato juice, *Campbell's®*

Salt and ground black pepper

Green jalapeño hot sauce, *Tabasco®*

Saltine crackers, *Nabisco®*

1. In a large microwave steaming cooking bag, on high setting (100 percent power), heat snapper fillets in an even layer in a microwave oven for 4 minutes. Chill fish in the refrigerator for 1 hour.

2. Cut the shrimp and fish into ½-inch pieces and toss with the dressing mix in a glass bowl. Stir in the lime juice and soda. Add the onion, avocado, garlic, jalapeños, and cilantro. Cover the surface with plastic wrap; refrigerate for 2 to 4 hours. (The shrimp are "cooked" when they turn pink and are opaque; fish should be opaque.) Drain and discard liquid. Stir in the tomato juice and season with salt and pepper. Add a few drops of hot sauce. Serve in stemmed glasses or beer mugs with saltine crackers.

Parmesan Polenta

Prep 15 minutes   **Bake** 20 minutes   **Servings** 14 servings

No-stick cooking spray, *Pam®*

¾ **cup white beans,** *S&W®*

1 **teaspoon crushed garlic,** *Gourmet Garden®*

2 **tablespoons grated Parmesan cheese,** *DiGiorno®*

1 **tube (24-ounce) prepared polenta,** *San Gennaro®*

4 **tablespoons plus 2 teaspoons refrigerated pesto sauce,** *Buitoni®*

3 **tablespoons diced pimientos,** *Dromedary®*

1. Preheat oven to 375 degrees F. Spray a baking sheet with cooking spray; set aside.

2. In a food processor, process beans, garlic, and Parmesan until it's a paste; set aside. Trim ends of polenta; discard trimmings. Cut polenta into ½-inch slices. Using a 1½-inch circle cookie cutter, cut polenta into 14 circles. Place on prepared baking sheet. Bake in preheated oven for 10 minutes. Spoon ½ teaspoon of the white bean mixture and ½ teaspoon of the pesto on polenta slices. Top with diced pimientos. Return to oven and bake for another 10 minutes.

Blue Cheese Shrimp Bites

Prep 10 minutes   **Bake** 15 minutes   **Makes** 16 servings

6 **ounces blue cheese, cut into 16 pieces and frozen**

8 **slices bacon, cut in half**

16 **large cooked shrimp (16 to 20 count)**

¼ **cup herb and garlic marinade,** *Lawry's®*

1. Preheat the oven to 425 degrees F. Line a baking pan with foil; set aside.

2. Place a piece of the cheese on one end of bacon strip. Place a shrimp on top. Roll tightly. Arrange shrimp on the prepared baking pan and brush generously with the marinade. Bake in the preheated oven for 15 to 20 minutes or until bacon is crisp.

Beer and Cheddar Pretzel Dip

Prep 5 minutes   **Cook** 10 minutes   **Bake** 15 minutes   **Makes** 10 servings

No-stick cooking spray, *Pam®*

1   **can (10.7-ounce) condensed cheddar cheese soup,** *Campbell's®*

1   **package (8-ounce) cream cheese, softened,** *Philadelphia®*

2   **tablespoons horseradish mustard,** *Inglehoffer®*

½   **package (0.4-ounce) buttermilk ranch dressing mix,** *Hidden Valley®*

1   **bottle (12-ounce) pale beer,** *Budweiser®*

2   **cups finely shredded sharp cheddar cheese,** *Sargento®*

Warm soft pretzels

1. Preheat oven to 350 degrees F.

2. Spray a 1-quart oven safe baking dish with cooking spray. In a medium saucepan, over medium-high heat, cook and stir together the cheddar cheese soup, cream cheese, mustard, and ranch dressing mix until the cream cheese has melted. Stir in the beer. Remove from the heat and add the cheddar cheese, a handful at a time, stirring until thoroughly combined. Transfer cheese mixture to the prepared baking dish and bake for 15 to 20 minutes or until bubbly. Serve with warm soft pretzels.

Parmesan Rolls 3 Ways

Prep 10 minutes   **Bake** 15 minutes   **Makes** 12 rolls

No-stick cooking spray, *Pam*®

1   roll (11-ounce) refrigerated breadstick dough, *Pillsbury*®

2   tablespoons butter, melted

3   tablespoons shredded Parmesan cheese, *DiGiorno*®

VARIATION 1: GARLIC BUTTER MOZZARELLA

1   tablespoon butter, melted

1   tablespoon garlic spread concentrate, *Lawry's*®

¼   cup shredded mozzarella cheese, *Kraft*®

VARIATION 2: PESTO

2   tablespoons prepared pesto, *Buitoni*®

VARIATION 3: SUN-DRIED TOMATO

2   tablespoons prepared sun-dried tomato pesto, *Buitoni*®

1. Preheat oven to 375 degrees F. Lightly spray an 8-inch round cake pan with cooking spray; set aside. Separate breadsticks.

2. For Variation 1, in a small bowl, combine butter, garlic concentrate, and cheese. Spread filling on individual breadsticks. (For Variation 2 or Variation 3, spread ingredients on individual breadsticks.) Roll up breadsticks and place in the prepared pan. Using a pastry brush, brush tops with melted butter and sprinkle with Parmesan cheese. Bake in preheated oven for 15 to 18 minutes, or until golden brown.

Pineapple Sweet Potato Kabobs

Prep 15 minutes   Bake 30 minutes   Makes 18 kabobs

¼   cup brown sugar, *Domino®/C&H®*

½   teaspoon ground nutmeg, *McCormick®*

1   teaspoon salt-free lemon-pepper seasoning, *The Spice Hunter®*

1   package (8-ounce) cut sweet potatoes, *Earth Exotic®*

2   tablespoons vegetable oil

1   package (8-ounce) pineapple chunks, cut in half diagonally for 18 pieces, *Ready Pac®*

6   tablespoons hazelnuts

3   tablespoons soft chèvre cheese, *Silver Goat®*

1. Preheat oven to 375 degrees F. Line a baking sheet with foil; set aside.

2. In a small bowl, stir together brown sugar, nutmeg, and lemon-pepper seasoning. Place sweet potatoes on baking sheet. Drizzle with oil and toss to coat. Sprinkle 1 tablespoon of seasoning mixture over sweet potatoes and toss until thoroughly coated. Place sweet potatoes on one half of the baking sheet. Bake in preheated oven for 20 minutes. Add pineapple to the other half of the baking sheet and sprinkle with remaining seasoning mixture. Bake for another 10 to 15 minutes or until sweet potatoes are tender and the pineapple is warm. Cool on a wire rack.

3. In a food processor, process hazelnuts to fine crumbs; pour into a pie plate. Shape ½ teaspoon cheese into a ball; roll in hazelnuts. Repeat to make 18 cheese balls. On 18 wooden toothpicks, thread pineapple, cheese, and sweet potatoes.

Farm Stand Tomato Tart

Prep 15 minutes   Bake 20 minutes   Makes 4 servings

2   tablespoons shredded Parmesan cheese, *DiGiorno*®

2   teaspoons Italian seasoning, *McCormick*®

1   sheet puff pastry, *Pepperidge Farm*®

1   small red onion, sliced

2   roma tomatoes, sliced

¼   cup real crumbled bacon bits, *Hormel*®

1   tablespoon extra virgin olive oil

1. Preheat oven to 400 degrees F. Line a baking sheet with parchment paper; set aside.

2. In a small bowl, combine Parmesan cheese and Italian seasoning; set aside. Unroll pastry. Using a sharp knife, score a ½-inch border around the pastry. Using a fork, prick the inner rectangle of the pastry. Arrange onions and tomatoes in the center of puff pastry. Sprinkle with bacon bits; drizzle with the olive oil. Sprinkle with Parmesan cheese mixture. Bake in preheated oven for 20 to 25 minutes or until pastry is golden brown and cheese has melted.

Taste of Italy

One of my favorite places in the world is the neighborhood in New York City known as Little Italy. The sights, sounds, and—especially—the smells are so enticing: a wood-burning pizza oven, Italian pastries baking, espresso being brewed. If you can't get to New York—or Italy—any time soon, these hearty dishes will transport you there.

Supreme Sicilian Lasagna

Prep 30 minutes   **Cook** 7 minutes   **Bake** 55 minutes   **Rest** 15 minutes   **Makes** 12 servings

No-stick cooking spray, *Pam®*

FOR THE LASAGNA:

1	pound lean ground beef
1	cup diced onions, *Ready Pac®*
2	containers (15 ounces each) ricotta cheese, *Sargento®*
2	large eggs
1	tablespoon Italian seasoning, *McCormick®*
¼	teaspoon kosher salt
4	cups shredded Italian cheese blend, *Sargento®*
1¼	cups shredded sharp cheddar cheese, *Sargento®*
1	box (9-ounce) no-boil lasagna noodles, *Barilla®*

FOR THE SAUCE:

2	jars (26 ounces each) mushroom and ripe olive pasta sauce, *Classico®*
¼	cup Marsala wine
1	tablespoon garlic blend, *Gourmet Garden®*
	Salt and ground black pepper
	Fresh chopped flat-leaf parsley, (optional)

1. Preheat oven to 375 degrees F. Spray a 9×13-inch baking dish with cooking spray; set aside.

2. For the lasagna, in a large skillet, over medium-high heat, brown ground beef, stirring frequently to break into small pieces. Add onions and cook and stir for 2 minutes or until tender. Remove from heat; set aside. In a large bowl, stir together ricotta, eggs, Italian seasoning, salt, 3 cups of the Italian cheese blend, and ½ cup cheddar cheese; set aside.

3. For the sauce, in a large bowl, stir together pasta sauce, wine, and garlic until smooth. Season to taste with salt and pepper.

4. To assemble, spoon 1 cup sauce in bottom of prepared baking dish. Arrange 4 noodles in single layer over sauce, breaking noodles if necessary. Spread half of beef and onions over top of noodles. Spread half of ricotta mixture over beef. Top with 4 more noodles, 1 cup sauce, remaining half of beef and onions, and remaining half of ricotta. Top with 4 more noodles, remaining sauce, remaining 1 cup of the Italian cheese blend, and remaining ¾ cup cheddar cheese. Cover tightly with foil. Bake in preheated oven for 45 to 50 minutes. Remove foil and bake another 10 minutes or until top is lightly browned. Remove and let sit 15 minutes before cutting to serve. Garnish with chopped parsley (optional).

Perfect Veal Piccata

Prep 10 minutes   **Cook** 10 minutes   **Makes** 4 servings

All-purpose flour

4   veal cutlets, pounded to ⅛-inch thickness

Salt

Lemon-pepper seasoning, *Lawry's*®

3   tablespoons extra virgin olive oil

2   teaspoons chopped garlic, *Gourmet Garden*®

1   cup dry white wine

¼   cup lemon juice, *Minute Maid*®

2   tablespoons capers, drained, *Delallo*®

2   tablespoons butter

¼   cup fresh finely chopped parsley

Lemon slices (optional)

Fresh parsley sprigs (optional)

1. Place flour in a shallow dish. Season both sides of the cutlets with salt and lemon-pepper seasoning. Coat cutlets in flour; pat off excess flour. In a large skillet, over medium-high heat, cook cutlets in hot oil for 2 minutes on each side. Transfer to a plate and keep warm. Add garlic to the skillet; cook and stir for 1 minute. Add wine to the skillet; bring to a boil and cook until reduced by half. Add lemon juice and capers and return to simmer. Stir in butter and parsley until the butter is melted. Return cutlets to the skillet and coat with the sauce. Transfer to a serving plate and top with remaining sauce. Garnish with lemon slices and parsley sprigs (optional).

Tuscan Roast Chicken

Prep 20 minutes   Bake 40 minutes   Makes 4 servings

No-stick cooking spray, *Pam*®

4   large lemons, thinly sliced

2   tablespoons chopped garlic, *Gourmet Garden*®

1   tablespoon lemon juice, *MinuteMaid*®

1½   teaspoons lemon-pepper seasoning, *Lawry's*®

5   tablespoons extra virgin olive oil

1   whole chicken, cut up, breasts cut in half

Salt and ground black pepper

1   bag (20-ounce) frozen roasted potatoes, *Ore-Ida*®

1   can (20-ounce) peeled Italian tomatoes, cut in half, undrained, *Hunts*®

2   medium zucchini, thinly sliced

20   pitted kalamata olives, *Marzetti*®

1   tablespoon fresh rosemary leaves, chopped

20   whole garlic cloves, *Christopher Ranch*®

½   cup Pecorino Romano cheese, *DiGiorno*®

1. Preheat oven to 400 degrees F. Spray a roasting pan with cooking spray. Line pan with lemon slices.

2. In a small bowl, stir together the chopped garlic, lemon juice, lemon-pepper seasoning, and 4 tablespoons of the olive oil; set aside. Place the chicken pieces on the lemon slices; lightly brush with the garlic-lemon mixture; reserve remaining garlic-lemon mixture. Season to taste with salt and pepper.

3. Toss potatoes with tomatoes, zucchini, olives, rosemary, and remaining 1 tablespoon olive oil until well coated. Using a slotted spoon, arrange vegetables and garlic cloves around chicken, reserving the liquid from the vegetables in case the pan dries out during baking. Bake for 20 minutes; brush with reserved garlic-lemon mixture and bake for another 20 to 25 minutes or until chicken registers 170 degrees F when tested with an instant-read thermometer, adding vegetable juices if necessary. Serve chicken with vegetables drizzled with pan juices and Pecorino Romano cheese.

Chicken Marsala

Prep 10 minutes   **Cook** 50 minutes   **Make** 4 servings

½   cup all-purpose flour

1   teaspoon salt

1   teaspoon ground black pepper

2   pounds bone-in chicken breasts, cut in half

1   tablespoon unsalted butter

2   tablespoons extra virgin olive oil, divided use

1   medium yellow onions, diced

2   tablespoons minced garlic, *Gourmet Garden*®

2   teaspoons bouillon chicken paste, *Better Than Bouillon*®

1   cup Marsala wine

1   packet (1.6-ounce) garlic and herb sauce mix, *Knorr*®

2   tablespoons chopped parsley (optional)

1. In a shallow pie pan, combine the flour, salt, and pepper. Coat chicken in the flour mixture, shaking off the excess.

2. In a large skillet, over high heat, melt the butter with 1 tablespoon olive oil. Cook the chicken for 10 minutes or until golden brown, turning once halfway through cooking. Remove chicken from pan; set aside. Reduce the heat to medium-high heat; add the remaining olive oil. Add onion and garlic; cook and stir for 4 minutes or until the onion is translucent. Add 1 cup *water,* bouillon, and wine; bring to a boil. Return the chicken to the skillet. Simmer, covered, for 30 to 45 minutes or until the internal temperature of the chicken reaches 170 degrees F. Place chicken on a platter; keep warm. Whisk the sauce mix into the skillet; bring to a boil, stirring constantly. Reduce heat and simmer for 3 minutes, stirring occasionally. Pour the sauce over the chicken. Sprinkle with parsley (optional).

Italian Baked Cod

Prep 15 minutes   **Bake** 15 minutes   **Makes** 4 servings

No-stick cooking spray, *Pam*®

2   cups **Italian seasoned bread crumbs**, *Progresso*®

¾   cup shredded **Parmesan cheese**, *DiGiorno*®

¾   cup minced **parsley**

3   teaspoons chopped **garlic**, *Garden Gourmet*®

2   teaspoons **Italian seasoning**, *McCormick*®

4   **cod fillets** (1½ pounds)

     Salt and ground black pepper

2   eggs

3   tablespoons **milk**

1   cup **flour**

6   tablespoons **extra virgin olive oil**

1   bag (16-ounce) frozen **broccoli florets**, *Birds Eye*®

¾   cup **tartar sauce**, *Hellmann's*® or *Best Foods*®

1   **lemon**, cut into wedges (optional)

1. Preheat oven to 425 degrees F. Line two rimmed baking sheets with aluminum foil and spray with cooking spray; set aside.

2. In a shallow bowl, mix the bread crumbs, Parmesan cheese, ½ cup of the parsley, 2 teaspoons garlic, and Italian seasoning. Reserve ⅓ cup; set aside.

3. Rinse cod and pat dry with paper towels. Season cod with salt and pepper. In a shallow dish, whisk together the eggs and milk. Place the flour in another shallow dish. Coat the fish in flour, shaking off the excess. Dip in the egg mixture and then coat in the bread crumb mixture. Place fish on prepared baking sheet. Drizzle with 3 tablespoons of the olive oil. Spread broccoli florets on the other prepared baking sheet and sprinkle with the reserved ⅓ cup bread crumbs. Drizzle broccoli with the remaining 3 tablespoons olive oil. Bake fish and broccoli for 15 to 20 minutes or until browned.

4. In a small bowl, stir together the tartar sauce, the remaining 1 teaspoon garlic, and reserved ¼ cup parsley. Serve fish with tartar sauce and garnish with lemon wedges (optional).

Crab Fra Diavolo

Prep 20 minutes   **Cook** 1 hour   **Makes** 4 servings

2	tablespoons extra virgin olive oil
1	yellow onion, chopped
2	tablespoons chopped garlic, **Gourmet Garden**®
2	cans (28 ounces each) crushed tomatoes, **Muir Glen**®
1	can tomato paste, **Muir Glen**®
1¾	cups water
1	bay leaf
1	package (½-ounce) fresh basil, stems removed, coarsely chopped
1	teaspoon fennel seeds, crushed
1	teaspoon red pepper flakes, **McCormick**®
2	pounds fresh or frozen king crab legs, meat removed, large shells reserved
	Kosher salt
1	pound bucatini pasta or thick spaghetti, cooked according to directions, **DeCeccho**®

1. In a stockpot, over medium-high heat, heat the oil. Add the onion and garlic; cook and stir for 5 minutes or until the onion is translucent. Add the tomatoes, and tomato paste, water, bay leaf, basil, fennel seeds, and red pepper flakes. Bring to a boil; add the reserved shells. Simmer, uncovered, for 30 minutes. Remove the shells; add the crabmeat and simmer for another 30 minutes. Remove and discard bay leaf before serving sauce with the pasta.

Note: The crab leg shells add great flavor to the dish. The crab leg shells are preslit, making it very easy to extract the meat. Don't use crab leg shells smaller than 3 inches for the sauce.

Tomato Basil Capellini

Prep 10 minutes   **Cook** 10 minutes   **Makes** 4 servings

¼   cup extra virgin olive oil

12   cloves garlic, *Christopher Ranch*®

1   can (28-ounce) petite diced
tomatoes, *Hunt's*®

1   teaspoon kosher salt

12   fresh basil leaves, torn into
dime-size pieces

1   box (16-ounce) capellini or angel
hair pasta, cooked according to
package directions, *DeCecco*®

1   cup part-skim ricotta, *Sargento*®

2   teaspoons Italian seasoning,
McCormick®

½   cup Parmesan cheese, *Sargento*®

1. In a medium skillet, over medium-high heat, heat 2 tablespoons of the olive oil. Add the garlic and cook and stir until the cloves are golden brown. Add the tomatoes and simmer, uncovered, for 5 minutes. Add the salt and torn basil. Toss the sauce with the pasta.

2. Place ricotta cheese in a microwave-safe container and stir in Italian seasoning. Cover and microwave on high setting (100 percent power) for 1 minute or until heated through, stirring after 30 seconds.

3. Place pasta on 4 individual serving plates and spoon ¼ cup ricotta cheese in the center. Sprinkle with Parmesan cheese and drizzle remaining 2 tablespoons olive oil over cheese.

Eggplant Rollatini

Prep 20 minutes   Stand 10 minutes   Bake 30 minutes   Makes 6 servings

No-stick cooking spray, *Pam®*

FOR THE EGGPLANT:

3   medium eggplants, sliced ½ inch thick lengthwise

Kosher salt

1   jar (25.5-ounce) tomato basil pasta sauce, *Barilla®*

FOR THE FILLING:

2   containers (15 ounces each) part-skim or whole milk ricotta cheese, *Sargento®*

1   package (16-ounce) shredded mozzarella and provolone cheese blend, *Sargento®*

¾   cup grated Parmesan cheese, *Sargento®*

2   teaspoons California-style garlic pepper with red bell and black pepper, *McCormick®*

¼   cup minced fresh flat-leaf parsley

2   large eggs, lightly beaten

Fresh basil leaves, torn (optional)

1. Preheat oven to 425 degrees F. Spray a 9×13-inch baking pan with cooking spray; set aside.

2. For the eggplant, place a wire cooling rack over a rimmed baking sheet. Lightly salt the eggplant slices on both sides and place them on the rack. Let sit for 10 minutes, then blot to remove excess moisture. Dry the baking sheet and spray with cooking spray. Bake on the prepared baking sheet for 10 minutes. Remove from oven and set aside to cool. Reduce oven temperature to 375 degrees F.

3. For the filling, in a large mixing bowl, mix the ricotta cheese, 2 cups of the mozzarella blend, ½ cup of the Parmesan cheese, garlic seasoning, and parsley. Stir in the eggs.

4. Place ¼ cup of the cheese mixture on the wide end of an eggplant slice and roll up tightly. Place each rollatini in the prepared baking pan, seamside down about 1 inch apart. Spoon some of the pasta sauce on top of each rollatini. Sprinkle with the remaining 2 cups mozzarella blend and the Parmesan cheese. Bake for 20 to 25 minutes or until the cheese melts and turns golden brown. Sprinkle with fresh basil (optional). Serve hot or at room temperature.

Risotto Carbonara

Prep 10 minutes   **Cook** 5 minutes   **Bake** 30 minutes   **Makes** 4 servings

2   teaspoons extra virgin olive oil

1   package (3-ounces) pancetta, chopped, *Columbus*®

1   cup frozen onions, *Ore-Ida*®

1   teaspoon crushed garlic, *Gourmet Garden*®

1   box (5.5-ounce) Italian herb risotto mix, *Lundberg*®

1½   cups chicken stock or broth, *Swanson*®

1   cup shredded Parmesan cheese, *DiGiorno*®

1   egg

1   egg yolk

1   tablespoon heavy cream

        Fresh chopped flat-leaf parsley (optional)

1. Preheat oven to 300 degrees F. In a large skillet, over medium-high heat, heat oil. Add pancetta and cook for 2 minutes. Remove pancetta from pan and set aside. Add onions and garlic and cook and stir for 2 minutes. Stir in risotto mix with seasoning packet and chicken stock. Bring to a boil; remove from heat. Return pancetta to skillet and cover with a lid or foil. Bake in preheated oven for 20 minutes. Stir in Parmesan cheese and bake for 10 to 12 minutes more or until all the stock is absorbed. Transfer risotto to a large serving bowl.

2. In a small bowl, whisk together egg, egg yolk, and heavy cream. Stir egg mixture into risotto until well combined and creamy. Garnish with flat-leaf parsley (optional).

Spinach Ricotta Tart

Prep 15 minutes   **Bake** 50 minutes   **Makes** 8 servings

2	refrigerated piecrusts, thawed, *Pillsbury*®
¾	cup egg substitute, *Egg Beaters*®
⅓	cup heavy cream
¾	cup ricotta cheese, *Precious*®
1	teaspoon citrus herb seasoning, *Spice Islands*®
½	teaspoon tarragon, *McCormick*®
1	package (10-ounce) frozen leaf spinach, thawed and squeezed dry, *C&W*®
1	jar (12-ounce) roasted red peppers, drained and chopped, *Delallo*®
	Salt and pepper
1	egg, lightly beaten with 1 teaspoon water

1. Preheat oven to 400 degrees F.

2. Press one piecrust into a 9-inch tart pan. Line the bottom and sides of the crust with foil. Place pie weights or dried beans on top of the foil. Bake in the preheated oven for 15 to 20 minutes. Remove the pie weights and foil. Cool the crust completely on a wire rack.

3. Meanwhile, on a lightly floured surface, roll out the other piecrust into a 10-inch circle, if necessary. Cut pastry into 1-inch-wide strips. On the back side of a baking sheet, weave strips in a lattice pattern. Cover with plastic wrap and refrigerate until ready to use.

4. Reduce oven temperature to 375 degrees F. In a large bowl, whisk together egg substitute, cream, ricotta cheese, citrus herb seasoning, and tarragon. Stir in spinach and red peppers; season with salt and pepper. Pour mixture into cooled piecrust. Brush egg wash around the edge. Place lattice crust over spinach filling. Pinch pastry edges together around the pan and trim any excess dough. Brush top of lattice with egg wash. Bake in the preheated oven for 35 to 40 minutes or until filling is set and crust is golden brown. Cool on a wire rack for 10 minutes before serving.

Fennel Baked Potatoes

Prep 10 minutes   **Bake** 35 minutes   **Makes** 4 servings

1	pound new potatoes, cut in half
4	tablespoons extra virgin olive oil
1½	teaspoons kosher salt
2	fennel bulbs, base and stems trimmed, fronds coarsely chopped
2	tablespoons Parmesan herb seasoning, *McCormick*®

1. Preheat oven to 375 degrees F. Toss the potatoes with 2 tablespoons of the olive oil and the salt. Spread evenly on a rimmed baking pan. Bake in the preheated oven for 30 to 35 minutes or until cooked through, stirring occasionally. Remove from the oven.

2. Meanwhile, using a vegetable peeler, shave the base of the fennel (the white part). Toss the fennel with the remaining 2 tablespoons olive oil. Increase the oven temperature to 475 degrees F. Add the fennel to the potatoes and bake for another 5 to 10 minutes or until the fennel is wilted and the potatoes are brown and crisp. Remove from the oven and toss with Parmesan herb seasoning. Garnish with the chopped fennel fronds.

Amazing Mexican

Creamy enchiladas, smoky fajitas, flaky chimichangas—so many of our favorite foods come from south of the border. These recipes have all the Latin flair of the traditional dishes that inspired them—but take just a fraction of the effort to make.

Lime Steak Fajitas

Prep 10 minutes   **Marinate** 24 hours   **Stand** 30 minutes   **Grill** 15 minutes   **Cook** 1 minute   **Makes** 4 servings

FOR THE FAJITAS:

8   ounces light lime vinaigrette, *Newman's Own® Lighten Up*

1   can diced green chiles, *Ortega®*

¼   cup soy sauce, *Kikkoman®*

2   tablespoons minced garlic, *Gourmet Garden®*

2   teaspoons coarsely ground black pepper

½   cup dark lager beer, *Samuel Adams® Black Lager*

2   pounds hanger or flank steaks

2   red bell peppers, cored, seeded, and halved lengthwise

     Vegetable oil

FOR ASSEMBLY:

1   package whole wheat tortillas (10-inch), *Mission® Whole Wheat Carb Balance*

1   tub (12-ounce) guacamole, *Calavo® Homestyle*

1   jar (16-ounce) green chile salsa, *Mrs. Renfro's®*

½   bunch fresh cilantro sprigs

1. Place vinaigrette, chiles, soy sauce, garlic, black pepper, and beer in a large zip-top bag. Squeeze out air and seal. Gently massage bag to combine ingredients. Add the steaks and red bell peppers to the bag. Marinate in the refrigerator for up to 24 hours, turning bag occasionally.

2. Set up grill for direct cooking over high heat. Oil the grate when ready to start cooking. Remove steaks and peppers from marinade; discard marinade. Grill the pepper halves about 9 minutes or until charred and softened, turning twice. Let steaks rest at room temperature for 20 to 30 minutes. Place steaks on hot oiled grill and cook for 4 minutes per side for rare (135 degrees F) or 6 minutes per side for medium-rare (145 degrees F). Transfer steaks to a platter and let stand 10 minutes before thinly slicing across the grain; slice peppers in eighths. Keep warm.

3. Place six tortillas at a time between paper towels. Microwave on high setting (100 percent power) for 30 to 40 seconds. To serve, fill warm tortillas with steak, peppers, guacamole, salsa, and rcilantro. Roll up tortillas.

Queso Blanco Skirt Steak

Prep 10 minutes   Cook 15 minutes   Stand 25 minutes   Grill 6 minutes   Makes 6 servings

FOR THE QUESO BLANCO:

1	cup shredded **Monterey Jack cheese**, *Sargento*®
2	tablespoons chopped **jalapeños**, *Ortega*®
6	tablespoons **half-and-half**
¼	cup diced **onion**, *Ready Pac*®
½	teaspoon ground **cumin**, *McCormick*®
⅛	teaspoon ground **coriander**, *McCormick*®
¼	teaspoon **kosher salt**
1	tablespoon chopped **fresh cilantro**

FOR THE SKIRT STEAK:

	Vegetable oil
2	pounds **skirt steak**
2	teaspoons **Montreal steak seasoning**, *McCormick*® *Grill Mates*
2	teaspoons **Mexican seasoning**, *The Spice Hunter*®

1. For the Queso Blanco, in a medium double boiler, over medium-high heat, cook and stir cheese, jalapeños, half-and-half, onion, cumin, coriander, salt, and cilantro for 15 minutes or until cheese is melted. Remove from heat; keep warm.

2. For the skirt steak, set up grill for direct cooking over high heat. Oil grate when ready to start cooking. Remove steak from the refrigerator and let stand for 20 minutes. Season both sides of steak with steak seasoning and Mexican seasoning. Place skirt steak on hot oiled grill and cook 3 to 5 minutes per side. Remove steak from grill and let rest 5 minutes. To serve, thinly slice skirt steak against the grain and top with warm Queso Blanco.

José Cuervo Margarita Beef

Prep 5 minutes   **Marinate** 2 hours   **Stand** 25 minutes   **Grill** 10 minutes   **Rest** 5 minutes   **Makes** 4 servings

2¾   **cups prepared golden margarita,** *José Cuervo*®

3   **tablespoons orange juice concentrate, thawed,** *Minute Maid*®

2   **tablespoons diced jalapeños,** *Ortega*®

4   **New York sirloins**

2   **fresh limes, thickly sliced**

     Vegetable oil

2   **large tomatoes, sliced ½ inch thick**

1. Place margarita, orange juice concentrate, and jalapeños in a zip-top bag. Squeeze out air and seal. Gently massage bag to combine ingredients. Add the steaks and limes. Marinate in refrigerator for at least 2 hours.

2. Set up grill for direct cooking over high heat. Oil grate when ready to start cooking. Remove steaks and limes from marinade; discard marinade. Let steaks sit at room temperature for 20 to 30 minutes. Place steaks on hot oiled grill. Cook for 4 to 6 minutes per side for rare (135 degrees F) or 6 to 8 minutes for medium (160 degrees F). Place tomatoes and reserved lime on grill. Cook for 2 minutes per side or until they have grill marks. Transfer steaks to a platter and let rest 5 minutes. Serve steaks with tomatoes and limes.

Poblano Rajas

Prep 5 minutes   **Cook** 18 minutes   **Makes** 4 servings

1   **tablespoon vegetable oil**

1   **medium yellow onion, sliced ½ inch thick**

1   **tablespoon minced garlic,** *Gourmet Garden*®

3   **cans (4-ounce) whole green chiles, sliced into ½-inch strips,** *Ortega*®

1   **cup Mexican crema,** *Cacique*®, **or crème fraiche or sour cream**

½   **teaspoon Mexican seasoning,** *The Spice Hunter*®

1   **bay leaf,** *McCormick*®

     Kosher salt

1. In a medium skillet, over medium-high heat, heat the oil. Add the onion and garlic and cook and stir for 6 to 7 minutes or until golden. Stir in chiles, crema, Mexican seasoning, and bay leaf. Simmer for 12 minutes or until thickened. Remove bay leaf. Season sauce to taste with salt. Serve as a condiment or a vegetable side dish with meats.

Chorizo-Crusted Pork Chops with Cheddar Mashers

Prep 20 minutes   Cook 7 minutes   Bake 25 minutes   Makes 4 servings

FOR THE CHOPS:

8	ounces Mexican chorizo sausage
½	cup bread crumbs, *Progresso®*
4	boneless center-cut pork chops, cut 1 inch thick
	Salt and ground black pepper
½	cup coarse-ground mustard, *Ingelhoffer®*

FOR THE SAUCE:

1	tablespoon olive oil
2	cups julienned yellow onions
1	tablespoon chopped garlic, *Gourmet Garden®*
2	tablespoons maple syrup, *Spring Tree®*
1	packet (1.2-ounce) au jus mix, *Knorr®*
1	can lower-sodium beef broth, *Swanson®*
	Salt and ground black pepper

FOR THE POTATOES:

1⅔	cups water
2	tablespoons butter
⅔	cup half-and-half
1¾	cups original mashed potato flakes, *Hungry Jack®*
3	ounces cream cheese, *Philadelphia®*
8	ounces shredded sharp cheddar cheese, *Sargento®*
¼	cup scallions, chopped

1. Preheat oven to 400 degrees F. Line a baking sheet with foil; set aside.

2. For the chops, remove chorizo from casing and place in a microwave-safe bowl. Cover and microwave on high heat setting (100 percent power) for 1 minute; stir. Cover and microwave for 30-second intervals until most of the fat is rendered; drain off fat. Add bread crumbs and stir to combine. Season chops with salt and pepper. Spread mustard on both sides of chops. Press chorizo onto the chops, coating both sides. Place chops on prepared baking sheet. Bake for 20 to 25 minutes or until internal temperature reaches 155 degrees F.

3. For the sauce, in a medium skillet, over medium-high heat, heat the oil. Add the onions and cook and stir for about 10 minutes or until onions are caramelized. Add garlic and cook for 1 minute more. In a medium bowl, stir together the maple syrup, au jus mix, and beef broth. Pour into skillet and bring to a boil. Reduce heat; simmer for 2 minutes, stirring occasionally. Season with salt and pepper.

4. For the potatoes, in a medium saucepan, over medium-high heat, bring the water, butter, and half-and-half to a boil. Add the potato flakes and stir with a fork until combined. Stir in the cream cheese, cheddar cheese, and 3 tablespoons of the scallions. Serve chops with sauce and potatoes. Garnish with the remaining scallions (optional).

New Mexico Roast Chicken

Prep 20 minutes   **Cook** 12 minutes   **Bake** 20 minutes   **Makes** 6 servings

No-stick cooking spray, *Pam®*

2 tablespoons extra virgin olive oil

1 large yellow onion, chopped

3 tablespoons minced garlic, *Gourmet Garden®*

2 medium zucchini, chopped

1 medium yellow squash, chopped

1 cup corn kernels, thawed, *Green Giant®*

1 can (10-ounce) diced tomatoes and green chiles, *Ro-Tel®*

1 tube (16-ounce) prepared polenta, diced, *San Gennaro®*

2 cups shredded cheddar-Jack cheese blend, *Sargento®*

1 tablespoon Mexican seasoning, *The Spice Hunter®*

3 teaspoons garlic salt, *Lawry's®*

6 boneless, skinless chicken breasts

3 scallions, sliced (optional)

1. Preheat oven to 400 degrees F. Spray a 9×13-inch baking dish with cooking spray; set aside.

2. In a large skillet, over medium-high heat, heat the oil. Add the onion and garlic and cook for 30 seconds. Add zucchini, yellow squash, and corn; cook and stir for 10 minutes or until the vegetables are tender. Add tomatoes and cook for another 2 to 3 minutes or until heated through. Remove from heat. Stir in polenta and cheese. Spoon into the prepared baking dish; set aside.

3. In a small bowl, combine Mexican seasoning and garlic salt. Sprinkle mixture on both sides of the chicken. Place chicken on top of vegetable mixture in baking dish. Bake in preheated oven for 20 minutes or until vegetable mixture is bubbly and chicken is cooked through. Remove from oven and sprinkle with scallions (optional).

Drunken Jalapeño-Peach Chicken

Prep 10 minutes   **Marinate** 1 hour   **Cook** 2 minutes   **Bake** 50 minutes   **Makes** 4 servings

No-stick cooking spray, *Pam*®

4	pounds meaty chicken pieces
¾	cup gold tequila, *José Cuervo*®*
¾	cup peach nectar, *Kern's*®
1	teaspoon salt
1	teaspoon ground black pepper
1	jar (10-ounce) peach fruit spread, *Polaner*®
4	tablespoons jalapeño jelly, *Tabasco*®
1	tablespoon diced jalapeños, minced, *Ortega*®
1	tablespoon chopped garlic, *Gourmet Garden*®

1. Preheat oven to 350 degrees F. Spray a baking sheet with cooking spray; set aside.

2. Place chicken in a large zip-top bag with ½ cup tequila and ½ cup peach nectar. Squeeze out air and seal. Gently massage bag to combine ingredients. Marinate in the refrigerator for 1 hour or up to 4 hours. Remove chicken from marinade; discard marinade. Season with salt and pepper. Place chicken pieces on prepared baking sheet at least 1 inch apart.

3. In a small saucepan, over medium-low heat, heat the remaining ¼ cup tequila, remaining ¼ cup peach nectar, peach spread, jalapeño jelly, jalapeños, and garlic, stirring occasionally, until the jelly melts. Baste chicken with the glaze. Bake for 10 minutes and baste chicken. Bake for another 30 minutes and baste again. Bake for another 10 minutes or until golden brown. (If the chicken gets brown too quickly, cover loosely with foil.)

*Note: May substitute peach nectar for the tequila if you like.

Chicken Ranch-ilada Bake

Prep 30 minutes   Bake 30 minutes   Makes 6 servings

No-stick cooking spray, *Pam*®

1   can (28-ounce) green enchilada sauce, *Las Palmas*®

1½   cups shredded rotisserie chicken

½   cup frozen chopped onions, *Ore-Ida*®

1   cup sour cream

1   packet (1-ounce) ranch dressing mix, *Hidden Valley*®

1   can (4-ounce) diced green chiles, *Ortega*®

3   cups shredded pepper Jack cheese, *Sargento*®

½   cup canola oil or corn oil

12   corn tortillas, *Mission*®

Mexican crema or sour cream

1. Preheat oven to 350 degrees F. Lightly spray 9×13-inch baking dish with cooking spray; set aside.

2. Spread 1 cup enchilada sauce on bottom of baking dish; set aside. In large bowl, stir together chicken, onions, sour cream, dressing mix, chiles, and 2 cups shredded cheese; set aside.

3. In a medium skillet, over medium-high heat, heat oil. Fry tortillas flat, one at a time, about 5 seconds per side, so they are still pliable. Use tongs to remove from skillet; drain on paper towel-lined plate. Dip tortillas into enchilada sauce. Spoon about ¼ cup of the chicken mixture onto each tortilla near the edge; roll up. Place filled tortillas, seam sides down, in the prepared baking dish. Pour remaining sauce over the enchiladas; sprinkle with remaining cheese. Bake in preheated oven for 30 to 35 minutes or until heated through. Drizzle with crema; serve.

Chicken Chimichangas
with Pineapple Salsa

Prep 20 minutes   Bake 25 minutes   Makes 4 servings

FOR THE CHIMICHANGAS:

No-stick cooking spray, *Pam®*

1   rotisserie chicken, shredded

1   jar (16-ounce) green salsa,
     Mrs. Renfro's®

2   teaspoons ground cumin,
     McCormick®

1   can (15-ounce) refried black beans,
     Rosarita®

1   package whole wheat flour
     tortillas (10-inch), *Mission® Whole
     Wheat Carb Balance*

1   bunch scallions, sliced

1   package (16-ounce) shredded
     Mexican cheese blend, *Sargento®*

FOR THE SALSA:

1   can (8-ounce) pineapple tidbits,
     drained, *Dole®*

1   can (8-ounce) crushed pineapple,
     Dole®

½   cup finely chopped fresh cilantro

     Pickled jalapeño pepper slices
     (optional)

1. Preheat oven to 425 degrees F. Spray a baking sheet with cooking spray; set aside.

2. For the chimichangas, in a mixing bowl, combine chicken, ¾ cup salsa, and cumin; set aside. On a clean working surface, spoon 2 tablespoons refried beans onto a tortilla, just below the center of the tortilla, leaving a 2-inch border. Top with ¼ cup of the chicken mixture, some scallions, and ¼ cup cheese. Fold the bottom edge of each tortilla up and over the filling. Fold opposite sides in and over the filling. Roll up from the bottom. Arrange chimichangas, seam sides down, on the prepared baking sheet 1 inch apart. Spray each chimichanga with cooking spray. Bake for 25 minutes or until golden brown.

3. For salsa, in a medium bowl, combine the remaining 1¼ cups salsa, pineapple tidbits, crushed pineapple, and cilantro.

4. Serve chimichangas with salsa and garnish with jalapeño slices (optional).

Salsa Chicken Bake

Prep 15 minutes **Bake** 25 minutes **Makes** 6 servings

No-stick cooking spray, *Pam*®

½ bag (16-ounce) yellow corn tortilla chips, slightly crushed, *Mission*®

1 bag (20-ounce) frozen fully cooked oven-roasted diced chicken breast, thawed, *Tyson*®

3 tablespoons mesquite seasoning, *McCormick*® *Grill Mates*®

1 jar (16-ounce) salsa, *Newman's Own*®

1 cup light sour cream

1 can (4-ounce) diced green chiles, *Ortega*®

1 cup pimiento-stuffed olives, rinsed, *Early California*®

½ cup chopped fresh cilantro

4 cups shredded Mexican cheese blend, *Kraft*®

1 cup low-sodium chicken broth, *Swanson*®

1. Preheat oven to 350 degrees F. Spray a 9×13-inch baking pan with cooking spray; set aside.

2. Pour the broken chips into the baking dish; set aside. In a large bowl, thoroughly combine the chicken with the mesquite seasoning; set aside. In a medium bowl, combine the salsa and sour cream. Stir in the chiles, olives, and cilantro. Stir salsa mixture into the chicken mixture. Add 3 cups of the cheese and the chicken broth. Spoon chicken mixture over the chips in the baking dish. Sprinkle remaining cheese. Bake for 25 to 35 minutes or until bubbly.

Green Chile Cheese Fudge

Prep 15 minutes **Bake** 35 minutes **Stand** 30 minutes **Makes** 12 servings

No-stick cooking spray, *Pam*®

1 bag (2 pounds) shredded Mexican cheese blend, *Sargento*®

8 ounces shredded Oaxaca cheese

2 cans (4.5 ounces each) chopped green chiles, *Ortega*®

1 tablespoon garlic blend, *Gourmet Garden*®

½ cup chopped fresh cilantro

½ cup sliced scallions

4 fresh jalapeños, cored, seeded, and minced

1 package (8-ounce) cream cheese, cubed, *Philadelphia*®

2 eggs

1 can (12-ounce) evaporated milk, *Carnation*®

½ cup all-purpose flour

1. Preheat oven to 350 degrees F. Spray 9×13-inch baking pan with cooking spray.

2. In a large bowl, combine the cheese blend, Oaxaca cheese, chiles, garlic, cilantro, scallions, and jalapeños. Toss cream cheese with the cheese mixture; set aside. In a small bowl, beat together the eggs, milk, and flour. Add to cheese mixture and stir. Pour into prepared pan. Bake in preheated oven for 35 to 45 minutes or until set. Transfer to a wire rack to cool until warm but not hot. Invert onto a baking sheet. Cover; refrigerate. To serve, cut into squares. Serve as an appetizer, as part of a cheese plate, or addition as an to a salad.

Enchiladas del Mar

Prep 10 minutes   **Cook** 25 minutes   **Bake** 20 minutes   **Makes** 6 servings

No-stick cooking spray, *Pam*®

1 tablespoon extra virgin olive oil

¼ cup minced yellow onion

2 teaspoons chopped garlic, *Gourmet Garden*®

12 large shrimp, peeled, deveined

8 ounces bay scallops

½ cup dry white wine

3 packages (3.5-ounce) premium crabmeat, *Chicken of the Sea*®

2 cups heavy cream

1 cup salsa verde, *La Victoria*®

Kosher salt and ground black pepper

12 corn tortillas, *Mission*®

8 ounces cream cheese, softened, *Philadelphia*®

4 cups grated Monterey Jack cheese, *Sargento*®

18 sprigs fresh cilantro

¼ cup pickled jalapeño slices, *Ortega*®

1 avocado, pitted, peeled, and sliced

1. Preheat oven to 350 degrees F. Lightly spray a 9×13-inch baking pan with cooking spray; set aside.

2. In a large skillet, over medium-high heat, heat oil. Add onion and garlic and cook and stir for 5 minutes or until onions are translucent. Add the shrimp and scallops; cook and stir for another minute. Add the wine and cook 3 minutes more or until the wine is almost evaporated. Transfer seafood to a medium bowl and add crabmeat. Add cream and salsa verde to the skillet and simmer for about 8 minutes or until thickened. Add seafood mixture to sauce and warm through. Season with salt and pepper. Transfer seafood mixture to a bowl; keep warm. Wipe out skillet.

3. In the same skillet, lightly toast tortillas over high heat. Place tortillas on a clean work surface. Spread each tortilla with cream cheese. Spoon about ¼ cup of the Monterey Jack cheese onto each tortilla near the edge and top with 2 sprigs of cilantro; roll up. Place filled tortillas, seam sides down, in the prepared baking dish; spoon seafood sauce over enchiladas. Sprinkle with remaining Monterey Jack cheese and jalapeños. Bake in preheated oven for 20 minutes or until heated through. Serve with avocado and remaining cilantro sprigs.

Comfort Food Favorites

Sometimes you need the culinary equivalent of a big warm hug. After you've polished off a plate of crispy Oven-Fried Chicken and Gravy and Savory Sausage Cheese Grits—topped off with creamy, sweet Caramel Cream Pots—you can't help feeling better.

French-Onion Salisbury Steak
on Texas Cheese Toast

Prep 10 minutes   Broil 10 minutes   Cook 2 minutes   Bake 15 minutes   Makes 6 servings

2   packets (1 ounce each) beefy onion soup mix, *Lipton*®

2   pounds lean ground beef

½   cup bread crumbs, *Progresso*®

2   teaspoons herbes de Provence, *The Spice Hunter*®

1   teaspoon celery seeds, *McCormick*®

1   egg
      Salt and ground black pepper

1   teaspoon Worcestershire sauce, *Lea & Perrin's*®

1   teaspoon mustard powder, *Spice Islands*®

1   bag (12-ounce) sliced Swiss cheese, *Sargento*®

1   box (9.5-ounce) five-cheese Texas toast, toasted according to package directions, *Pepperidge Farm*®

1. Preheat broiler. Line a rimmed baking sheet with foil; set aside.

2. In a large bowl, mix together 1 packet soup mix, ground beef, bread crumbs, herbes de Provence, celery seeds, and egg. Season with salt and pepper. Form into 6 oval-shape patties. Place the patties on the prepared baking sheet and broil 4 inches from the heat for 5 minutes or until browned. Turn patties over and broil for 5 more minutes. Remove baking sheet from broiler and cover with foil to keep patties warm. Preheat oven to 375 degrees F.

3. In a large ovenproof skillet, over high heat, combine remaining soup mix with 2 cups *water*. Remove from heat and add Worcestershire sauce and mustard. Place broiled patties in the skillet with the sauce. Place skillet in the oven and bake for 8 to 10 minutes or until internal temperature reaches 145 degrees F. Remove pan from oven; top each patty with 3 slices of cheese and bake for 8 minutes more or until cheese is softened.

4. To serve, place a piece of toast on a serving plate or in a shallow soup bowl and top with a patty. Spoon sauce around the patty.

Simplest Peach Chops
and Poppy Seed Coleslaw

Prep 10 minutes   Cook 10 minutes   Makes 6 servings

FOR THE PEACH CHOPS:

1	teaspoon salt
½	teaspoon ground black pepper
6	boneless pork chops, cut 1 inch thick
2	tablespoons olive oil
½	cup peach preserves, *Smucker's*®
2	tablespoons Dijon mustard, *Grey Poupon*®
1	tablespoon water

FOR THE POPPY SEED COLESLAW:

1	bag (16-ounce) tri-color coleslaw mix, *Fresh Express*®
1	can (8.25-ounce) mandarin oranges, drained, *Del Monte*®
1	can (8-ounce) pineapple chunks, drained, *Dole*®
½	cup poppy seed dressing, *Knott's*®
½	cup organic sour cream, *Horizon*®

1. Rub salt and pepper on both sides of the chops. In a medium skillet, over medium-high heat, heat the oil. Add the chops and cook for 2 minutes on each side or until browned. Reduce the heat to medium; add preserves, mustard, and water. Cook, covered, for 3 to 4 minutes on each side or until the internal temperature reaches 150 degrees F.

2. For the poppy seed coleslaw, in a large bowl, combine coleslaw mix, mandarin oranges, and pineapple; set aside. In a small bowl, stir together the dressing and sour cream. Pour over coleslaw mixture and toss to coat. Chill until ready to serve.

Barbecued Pulled Pork
with Pickled Red Onions

Prep 20 minutes   **Stand** 5 minutes   **Chill** 2 hours   **Cook** 8 hours (Low)   **Rest** 5 minutes   **Makes** 8 servings

**FOR THE PICKLED
RED ONIONS:**

1 ½   cups boiling water

1   red onion, halved, thinly sliced

2   jalapeños, cored and seeded, cut into julienne strips

1   cup grape juice, *Welch's*®

⅓   cup cider vinegar, *Heinz*®

1   teaspoon kosher salt

**FOR THE MUSTARD
BBQ SAUCE:**

¼   cup stone-ground mustard, *Inglehoffer*®

2   tablespoons minced garlic, *Gourmet Garden*®

½   cup cider vinegar, *Heinz*®

¼   cup honey, *Sue Bee*®

1   cup hickory-flavored barbecue sauce, *Bulls-Eye*®

FOR THE PORK ROAST:

1   3- to 4-pound pork shoulder roast

2   teaspoons kosher salt

1   teaspoon ground black pepper

8   kaiser rolls

1. For the pickled onions, in a small bowl, pour boiling water over the sliced onion and jalapeños. Let stand 5 minutes; drain and rinse with cold water. Return jalapeños and onion to the bowl; toss with grape juice, vinegar, and salt. Cover and chill at least 2 hours.

2. For the sauce, in a small saucepan, over medium heat, cook and stir the mustard, garlic, vinegar, honey, and barbecue sauce for 10 minutes. Remove from heat; set aside.

3. For the pork roast, rinse the pork roast and dry with paper towels. Rub the salt and pepper all over the roast. Place roast in the slow cooker and add the Mustard BBQ Sauce.

4. Cook on Low for 8 to 10 hours.

5. Transfer meat to a cutting board or platter and let rest for 5 minutes. Using two forks, pull meat apart into shreds. Strain sauce and add 1 cup to the shredded pork. Serve pork with the pickled onions on rolls with extra sauce on the side.

Sausage-Stuffed Peppers and Cabbage

Prep 20 minutes   **Bake** 1 hour   **Makes** 6 servings

8	large cabbage leaves
1	medium red bell pepper
1	medium green bell pepper
1	pound mild Italian sausage, *Johnsonville*®
1	pound lean ground beef
½	cup converted rice, *Uncle Ben's*®
1	cup frozen chopped onions, thawed, *Ore-Ida*®
1	packet (1.5-ounce) meat loaf seasoning, *McCormick*®
1	packet (0.5-ounce) pesto sauce mix, *Knorr*®
2	eggs
1	jar (26-ounce) pasta sauce, *Newman's Own*®
2	cans (14.5 ounces each) diced tomatoes with green peppers, celery, and onion, *Hunt's*®

1. Preheat oven to 350 degrees F.

2. Place cabbage leaves in a large bowl and cover with boiling water; set aside to wilt. Cut red and green bell peppers into fourths through the stem ends. Remove seeds and membranes; set aside.

3. In a large bowl, stir together the sausage, ground beef, uncooked rice, onions, meat loaf seasoning, pesto mix, and eggs; set aside. Spoon ¼ cup of the meat mixture onto the bell peppers. Place peppers in a 9×13-inch pan, alternating colors and leaving a space for the cabbage rolls. Remove cabbage leaves from the water and cut off the thickest part. Spoon ¼ cup of the meat mixture onto the center of each leaf. Fold over sides and roll up. Place cabbage rolls between the peppers (use an additional pan if necessary).

4. In a small bowl, stir together pasta sauce and diced tomatoes. Pour over peppers and cabbage. Cover with foil and bake in the preheated oven for 1 hour. Serve hot.

Super BBQ Chicken and Succotash

Prep 15 minutes   Bake 50 minutes   Cook 15 minutes   Makes 6 servings

No-stick cooking spray, *Pam*®

FOR THE BBQ CHICKEN:

4   pounds meaty chicken pieces

3   tablespoons mesquite seasoning, *McCormick® Grill Mates*

10   (5 inch) fresh rosemary sprigs

1   orange, sliced ¼ inch thick

1   bottle (16-ounce) barbecue sauce, *Stubb's*

2   tablespoons orange juice concentrate, *Minute Maid*®

FOR THE SUCCOTASH:

6   tablespoons unsalted butter

1   box (10-ounce) frozen lima beans, *Green Giant*®

4   tablespoons water

1   box (10-ounce) frozen corn, *Green Giant*®

1   jar (6.5-ounce) diced pimientos, drained, *Dromedary*®

2   tablespoons crumbled bacon, *Hormel*® (optional)

¾   cup cream

      Hot sauce, *Tabasco*®

      Kosher salt and ground black pepper

1. Preheat oven to 350 degrees F. Spray a rimmed baking pan with cooking spray; set aside.

2. Rub the chicken pieces with mesquite seasoning and place in the center of the prepared baking pan. Place 6 of the rosemary sprigs and the orange slices around the chicken. Bake in the preheated oven for 20 minutes.

3. Meanwhile, in a small bowl, combine the barbecue sauce and the orange juice concentrate. After the chicken has baked for 20 minutes, baste with the sauce. Bake for 30 to 35 minutes or until internal temperature reaches 160 degrees F, basting every 10 minutes.

4. For the succotash, in a medium saucepan, over medium-high heat, melt 4 tablespoons of the butter. Stir in lima beans and water. Cover and cook for 6 minutes. Add remaining 2 tablespoons of butter, corn, pimientos, and bacon pieces (optional). Stir in the cream and hot sauce; season with salt and pepper. Cook for 5 minutes or until heated through.

5. Serve the chicken with the succotash and baked orange slices. Garnish with the 2 remaining rosemary sprigs.

Oven-Fried Chicken and Ranch Gravy

Prep 15 minutes   **Stand** 15 minutes   **Bake** 45 minutes   **Cook** 5 minutes   **Makes** 4 servings

No-stick cooking spray, *Pam*®

FOR THE CHICKEN:

1	**sleeve saltine crackers, finely crushed,** *Nabisco*®
2	**whole eggs, lightly beaten**
⅓	**cup water**
	Ground black pepper
4	**pounds meaty chicken pieces**

FOR THE GRAVY:

2	**tablespoons butter**
1	**tablespoon all-purpose flour**
1	**tablespoon buttermilk ranch dressing mix,** *Hidden Valley*®
1	**cup less-sodium chicken broth,** *Swanson*®
1	**cup half-and-half**

1. Preheat oven to 425 degrees F. Spray a rimmed baking pan with cooking spray; set aside.

2. For the chicken, place the crackers in a shallow dish or pie plate. In a medium bowl, combine the eggs and water; season with pepper. Dip the chicken in the egg wash then coat both sides in the crackers. Set on the baking sheet about 1 inch apart. Let stand at room temperature for 15 minutes. Spray the chicken with cooking spray and bake for 45 to 50 minutes or until golden. Reserve 2 tablespoons pan drippings.

3. For the gravy, in a medium skillet, over medium heat, melt the butter. Add reserved pan drippings to skillet. Whisk in the flour and ranch dressing mix. Cook and stir until it turns a pale blond. Whisk in the broth; add the half-and-half and whisk until smooth. Serve gravy with the chicken.

Chicken Hash
with Country Gravy

Prep 10 minutes   Stand 5 minutes   Cook 20 minutes   Makes 6 servings

½   pound hot Italian sausage, casings removed

½   cup frozen chopped onions, *Ore-Ida*®

½   cup frozen chopped green peppers, *Pictsweet*®

2   tablespoons chopped pimientos, *Dromedary*®

1½   cups chicken broth, *Swanson*®

¼   cup butter

1   box (6-ounce) stuffing mix, *Stove Top*®

2   packages (6 ounces each) grilled chicken breast strips, finely chopped, *Foster Farms*®

2   tablespoons canola oil

1   packet (2.64-ounce) country gravy mix, *McCormick*®

1   cup cold milk

1   cup cold water

6   poached eggs

1. Heat a large skillet over medium-high heat; crumble sausage into skillet. Add onions, peppers, and pimientos and cook and stir for 6 to 8 minutes or until sausage is just cooked through. Transfer to a large bowl and wipe out the skillet.

2. In a medium saucepan, over medium heat, bring chicken broth and butter to a boil. Stir in stuffing mix with packet; cover. Remove from heat and let stand for 5 minutes. Fluff with a fork. Add to sausage mixture. Add chicken and mix well.

3. In the same skillet, over medium-high heat, heat oil. Add stuffing mixture to the pan; using a spatula, press into the skillet bottom. Cook for 5 to 7 minutes; do not touch. Use a spatula to turn over the hash and cook for another 5 to 7 minutes.

4. Meanwhile, in a medium saucepan, whisk together gravy mix, cold milk, and the water. Cook on medium heat until gravy comes to a boil, whisking occasionally. Reduce heat and simmer for 1 minute. Serve hash topped with poached eggs and warm gravy.

Split Cornish Hens
with Corn Bread Stuffing

Prep 15 minutes   Cook 20 minutes   Stand 5 minutes   Bake 30 minutes   Makes 4 servings

No-stick cooking spray, *Pam*®

FOR THE DRESSING:

2	tablespoons unsalted butter
1	yellow onion, diced
½	teaspoon celery seeds, crushed, *McCormick*®
½	teaspoon ground sage, *McCormick*®
1½	cups chicken broth, *Swanson*®
1	box (6-ounce) corn bread stuffing mix, *Stove Top*®

FOR THE HENS:

2	Cornish hens
2	tablespoons extra virgin olive oil
2	tablespoons unsalted butter, melted
¼	cup French herb roasting rub, *McCormick*®

FOR THE GRAVY:

½	cup dry white wine
1	can (10.75-ounce) cream of chicken with herbs soup, *Campbell's*®
2	tablespoons heavy cream
½	cup water

1. Preheat oven to 400 degrees F. Line two rimmed baking pans with foil and spray with cooking spray; set aside.

2. For the dressing, in a large saucepan, over medium-high heat, melt the butter. Cook and stir onions for 10 minutes or until translucent. Stir in the celery seeds, sage, and broth; bring to a boil. Add stuffing mix and packet. Cover, remove from heat, and let stand for 5 minutes. Fluff dressing with a fork. Using a large spoon, drop stuffing into 4 mounds onto the prepared baking pans; set aside.

3. For the hens, using kitchen shears, remove backbones from hens. Using a sharp knife, cut each hen in half through the breast, creating 4 pieces. In a small bowl, combine the oil and melted butter; rub mixture on both sides of hen pieces. Rub with the herb roasting rub. Place the hen pieces on the dressing; place baking pans in the oven and reduce the oven temperature to 350 degrees F. Bake for 30 to 40 minutes or until internal temperature reaches 160 degrees F, rotating the pans once halfway through cooking.

4. For the gravy, in a small saucepan, bring wine to a boil and cook for 5 minutes or until reduced by half. Add soup, cream, and water. Simmer for 5 minutes.

Savory Sausage Cheese Grits

Prep 15 minutes   Bake 15 minutes   Makes 4 servings

No-stick cooking spray, *Pam®*

4   breakfast sausage links, *Johnsonville®*

2   cups milk

¾   cup condensed cheddar cheese soup, *Campbell's®*

4   packets (1 ounce each) instant grits, *Quaker®*

½   cup frozen chopped onions, *Ore-Ida®*

½   cup crumbled bacon, *Hormel®*

½   cup shredded cheddar-Jack cheese, *Sargento®*

Salt and ground black pepper

4   tablespoons butter, cut into tiny pieces

1. Preheat oven to 350 degrees F. Spray four 4-inch ramekins with cooking spray; set aside.

2. In a medium skillet, over medium heat, cook breakfast sausage, breaking it up into small pieces. Remove from heat and drain fat; set aside.

3. In a large bowl, whisk together the milk and soup. Add the grits and whisk until smooth. Stir in the onions, bacon, cheese, and sausage. Season with salt and pepper. Spoon mixture into the prepared ramekins and top each with 1 tablespoon of butter pieces. Place ramekins on a baking sheet. Bake in preheated oven for 15 to 17 minutes or until heated through.

Praline Sweet Potato Casserole

Prep 15 minutes   Bake 45 minutes   Makes 6 servings

No-stick cooking spray, *Pam®*

FOR THE CASSEROLE:

3   cans (15 ounces each) cut sweet potatoes, drained, *Princella®*

3   large eggs, lightly beaten

½   cup (1 stick) unsalted butter, melted

1   can (5-ounce) evaporated milk, *Carnation®*, or ¼ cup heavy cream

2   teaspoons lemon juice, *Minute Maid®*

1   teaspoon vanilla extract, *McCormick®*

1   teaspoon pumpkin pie spice, *McCormick®*

FOR THE TOPPING:

1   cup packed light brown sugar, *Domino®/C&H®*

½   cup all-purpose flour

½   cup (1 stick) unsalted cold butter, cut in small pieces

2   cups finely chopped pecans, *Diamond®*

Pecan halves (optional)

1. Preheat oven to 350 degrees F. Spray a 9×13-inch baking pan with cooking spray; set side.

2. To make the casserole, in a large mixing bowl, mash the drained sweet potatoes with a potato masher. Stir in the eggs. Add the butter, evaporated milk, lemon juice, vanilla extract, and pumpkin pie spice; mix until well combined. Spread into the prepared baking pan.

3. To make the topping, in a medium bowl, combine the sugar and flour. Using a pastry blender, cut in the butter until mixture is the size of peas. Stir in the chopped pecans. Sprinkle topping over the casserole. Garnish with pecan halves (optional). Bake for 45 minutes or until the top is browned.

Caramel Cream Pots

Prep 15 minutes   **Chill** 4 hours   **Makes** 4 servings

3   **tablespoons liquid egg whites,** *Egg Beaters*®

¼   **cup milk**

3   **tablespoons butter, softened**

⅓   **cup heavy cream**

1   **bag (5.5-ounce) chewy caramels, unwrapped,** *Werther's Original*®

    Frozen whipped dessert topping, thawed, *Cool Whip*®

1. In a blender, process egg whites, milk, and butter until smooth. In a small saucepan, over medium-high heat, heat cream and caramels until completely melted, stirring constantly. Remove from heat and pour into blender. Process until smooth. Pour mixture into four 4-ounce ramekins. Cover each ramekin tightly with plastic wrap and chill in the freezer for 4 hours or until set. Serve with whipped topping.

Index

Sandra Lee Semi-Homemade Cookbook Series

Collect all of these smartly helpful, time-saving, and beautiful books by New York Times best-selling author and Food Network star, Sandra Lee.

sandralee.com

Sandra Lee has a passion for simple solutions that create dramatic results in all areas of home life. For exclusive recipes, time- and money-saving tips and tricks to make your home life easier, better and more enjoyable, log on to www.SandraLee.com. Sign up for the Semi-Homemaker's online club to receive free newsletters filled with fabulous recipes and great entertaining at-home ideas.

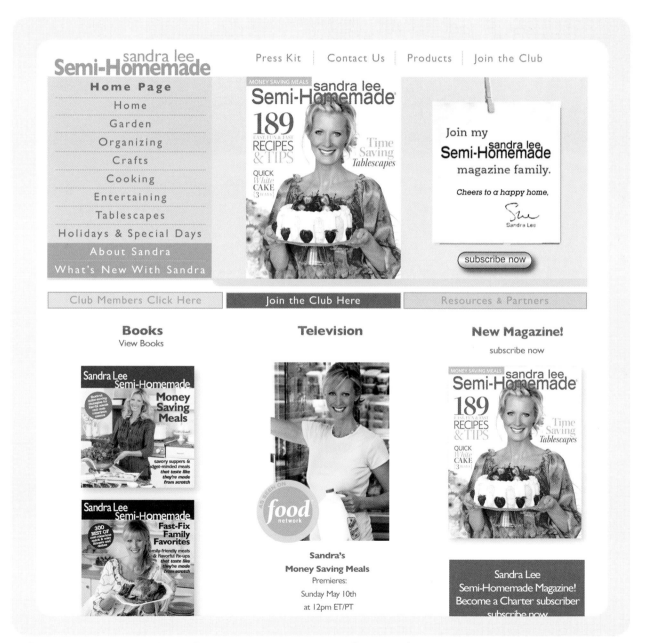

Go to SandraLee.com or Semihomemade.com

Making life easier, better, and more enjoyable